Early Intervention Progran
Opening the Door to Higher Educat

by Robert H. Fenske, Christine A. Geranios,
Jonathan E. Keller, and David E. Moore

ASHE-ERIC Higher Education Report Volume 25, Number 6

Prepared by

ERIC Clearinghouse on Higher Education
The George Washington University
URL: www.gwu.edu/~eriche

In cooperation with

Association for the Study
of Higher Education
URL: http://www.tiger.coe.missouri.edu/~ashe

Published by

Graduate School of Education and Human Development
The George Washington University
URL: www.gwu.edu

Jonathan D. Fife, Series Editor

Cite as

Fenske, Robert H., Christine A. Geranios, Jonathan E. Keller, and David E. Moore. 1997. *Early Intervention Programs: Opening the Door to Higher Education.* ASHE-ERIC Higher Education Report Volume 25, No. 6. Washington, D.C.: The George Washington University, Graduate School of Education and Human Development.

Library of Congress Catalog Card Number 97-73681
ISSN 0884-0040
ISBN 1-878380-78-8

Managing Editor: Lynne J. Scott
Manuscript Editor: Barbara Fishel/Editech
Cover Design by Michael David Brown, Inc., The Red Door
  Gallery, Rockport, ME

The ERIC Clearinghouse on Higher Education invites individuals to submit proposals for writing monographs for the *ASHE-ERIC Higher Education Report* series. Proposals must include:
1. A detailed manuscript proposal of not more than five pages.
2. A chapter-by-chapter outline.
3. A 75-word summary to be used by several review committees for the initial screening and rating of each proposal.
4. A vita and a writing sample.

ERIC Clearinghouse on Higher Education
Graduate School of Education and Human Development
The George Washington University
One Dupont Circle, Suite 630
Washington, DC 20036-1183

> *The mission of the ERIC system is to improve American education by increasing and facilitating the use of educational research and information on practice in the activities of learning, teaching, educational decision making, and research, wherever and whenever these activities take place.*

This publication was prepared partially with funding from the Office of Educational Research and Improvement, U.S. Department of Education, under contract no. ED RR-93-002008. The opinions expressed in this report do not necessarily reflect the positions or policies of OERI or the Department.

EXECUTIVE SUMMARY

The growth of early intervention programs reflects America's commitment to high levels of educational attainment for all citizens. This commitment is embodied in the national ideal of equal educational opportunity without regard to social or economic status. Early intervention programs offer new hope to youth who are disproportionately "at risk" of inadequate educational attainment by providing financial assistance and encouragement to them, their families, and their communities. An important goal of early intervention is to facilitate a seamless transition from elementary to secondary to higher education. To reach this goal, educators at all levels must develop and implement coordinated policies and planning strategies. Early intervention is aided by funds from federal agencies, state agencies, local governments, and philanthropic organizations.

What Is Early Intervention?

The number and diversity of programs providing services and resources to encourage low-income/minority youth to finish high school and enter college have been burgeoning since the early 1980s. The mission statement of the National Early Intervention Scholarship and Partnership program is a unifying concept for early intervention. The federal law encourages provision of financial assistance to low-income students to obtain high school diplomas and to foster the pursuit of higher education. The law also encourages states, local education agencies, community organizations, and private entities to provide a variety of information and support services for elementary, middle, and secondary students at risk of dropping out. These public and private agencies provide services, including mentoring, tutoring, and information, to help low-income and minority students obtain high school diplomas and seek admission to college. Many such programs attempt to eliminate the financial barriers to higher education by guaranteeing needed financial assistance for at-risk students if they graduate from high school and meet other criteria. The underlying assumption is that intervention early in the educational pipeline will help to prevent dropouts and increase the number of students who pursue higher education.

"Academic outreach" programs that originate in schools, colleges, and universities are a subset of the broader concept of early intervention. Academic outreach programs are differentiated from early intervention programs in that academic outreach programs are operated by academic institutions (although the source of funds and sponsor of the programs might be outside the institution). Although the distinctions between academic outreach and early intervention programs are imprecise, this distinction helps to identify the types of institutionally operated programs that can be directly affected by institutional faculty and administrators.

Academic outreach programs are similar in purpose to early intervention programs but are not always articulated or coordinated with them. The general purpose of most academic outreach programs is to encourage at-risk students to plan for college, with no focus on specific academic disciplines. Some academic outreach programs, however, focus on preparation and recruitment of promising at-risk students for selected academic disciplines. Academic outreach includes generally enhancing educational opportunity for underserved students within an institution's service area as well as increasing the number of at-risk students enrolled in specific academic disciplines. Thus, these programs are mutually beneficial to both underserved students and institutions of higher education.

A third type of approach to early intervention is the rapidly growing school-college collaboration movement, which involves systemic changes triggered by the reforms beginning in the early 1980s that attempt to close the traditional gap between K–12 and higher education. A new perspective, K–16, began to emerge in the 1980s in discussions of educational accountability. Early intervention programs that are built upon the collaborative efforts of K–12 and higher education institutions have gained momentum toward K–16 alliances. One of the most promising examples of such collaboration is the concept of "middle college," which melds the last two years of high school with the two years offered in public community colleges. Such alliances enhance the recruitment of minority students and increase the readiness of entering freshmen.

What Types of Early Intervention Programs Have Been Established?

Basically, early intervention programs take six forms: programs established by philanthropic agencies, federally supported programs, state-sponsored programs with matching federal support, entirely state-supported programs, systemic changes involving school-college collaboration, and college- or university-sponsored programs. In certain cases, programs began with private seed money from philanthropic organizations and later evolved into publicly sponsored programs. The many early intervention/academic outreach programs are varied and uncoordinated, and there is no national clearinghouse or database that tracks the growth of local, state, or federal programs.

What Are the Implications of the Growth of Early Intervention Programs for College and University Administrators?

Early intervention programs provide colleges and universities with a powerful tool to recruit disadvantaged students who need a broad base of support to enroll in and then graduate from college. By forming strong coalitions with schools and community leaders to collaborate in the development of innovative services and methods of delivery, higher education administrators can contribute to and capitalize on the wealth of offerings. Specifically, they can leverage institutional early intervention efforts by surveying the federal, state, regional, and local programs that can directly affect their institution, and by developing strategies and structures to coordinate institutional outreach programs with the multitude of early intervention programs that originate in both the public and private sectors. These developments can help overcome duplicative efforts and gaps in service caused by the current lack of coordination between institutions and programs.

Faculty members and administrators of colleges and universities recognize the importance of support from the public, from elected officials, and from philanthropic organizations, made evident in the recent trend toward the development of state "report cards" for higher education systems. One of the most common components of report cards is the assessment of access to public higher education, especially for underrepresented students. Institutions must demonstrate increased access to their institutions and success in the retention of diverse students. Colleges and universities must marshal and refine their resources to achieve these outcomes. Many institutions rely on remedial education to increase enrollments of students from underserved populations, but in many states, governors, legislators, and governing boards have criticized the need for postsecondary remedial education. Perhaps early intervention and academic outreach programs will enhance students' readiness and diminish the need for remedial education.

CONTENTS

Foreword	ix
Acknowledgments	xi
Introduction	1
Background	5
Early Intervention and Academic Outreach Defined	7
Why Intervene?	9
Private Initiatives	27
The I Have A Dream Foundation	28
A Better Chance	30
EQUITY 2000	31
American Indian Science and Engineering Society	32
Project WINGS	33
School-College Collaboration	35
The Traditional Separation between K–12 and Higher Education	35
The K–16 Movement	35
Federal and State-Supported Early Intervention	41
Early Federal Support	41
Federal and State Cost-Sharing Programs	43
State Implementation of NEISP	44
Other State Programs	48
Academic Outreach Programs	55
Two Surveys of Institutional Academic Outreach Programs	55
Two Institutional Examples of Academic Outreach	59
Community College Academic Outreach	68
Program Evaluation	73
Conclusions and Recommendations	81
Appendix: A Sample of Institutional Outreach Programs	87
References	93
Index	103
ASHE-ERIC Higher Education Reports	123
Advisory Board	125
Consulting Editors	127
Review Panel	129
Recent Titles	133
Order Form	

Institutions that participate in early intervention or academic outreach programs are institutions that are taking control of their futures. They are institutions that essentially are saying, "We are no longer willing to accept the luck of the draw on annual enrollments and are going to take a long-term, pro-active role in our future enrollments." Early intervention occurs when institutions or individual faculty members understand that by establishing early partnerships with K–12 institutions, they have the ability to redirect the lives of students who would otherwise not participate in higher education or in a particular area of study. It has been said that for children of upper-class families, higher education is an assumption and that for children of the middle class, higher education is an aspiration. But for many students, higher education is not even considered a remote possibility. It is the latter two groups that are the focus of early intervention programs.

Early intervention programs need to have a clear purpose to be successful. The traditional reason for such programs is for higher education faculty to help bring to K–12 institutions resources and expertise that would help encourage at-risk students to aspire to and work toward gaining a high school education that will allow them to go on to college. In helping develop such programs, college faculty are helping students develop their intellectual foundations before they are admitted to college and thereby reduce or eliminate the necessity for remedial programs.

Another objective for early intervention programs is to stimulate the interest of women and minorities in careers from which they have been historically excluded. Doing so may mean developing interests in such areas as mathematics and engineering or such professions as medicine and law. It may also mean attempting to start encouraging women and minorities at a very early age to think of the academy as a future career.

Another result of early intervention programs is a visible way for institutions to add value to their communities. Positive early intervention programs help to create better relationships between town and gown that promote the value of a higher education institution's fulfilling its social responsibilities.

Developing and supporting early intervention programs takes an understanding of the local community and careful planning by the institution. This report, by Robert H. Fenske, professor of higher education in the Division of Educational Leadership and Policy Studies at Arizona State University, Christine A. Geranios, coordinator of undergraduate studies for the Department of Communication at ASU, Jonathan E. Keller, a former policy analyst for the Arizona Board of Regents and current doctoral student at ASU, and David E. Moore, a graduate of ASU and student at Temple University School of Law, reviews the full scope of early intervention and academic outreach. The authors first establish a framework for these programs and then review the current federal and state involvement in helping institutions enter into early intervention programs with K–12 institutions. The authors conclude their report with specific examples of academic outreach programs at four-year colleges and universities and at community colleges.

Institutions may participate in early intervention programs because they believe it is their community responsibility or is part of a long-term strategy for managing enrollments. It may be done to develop better public relations, to decrease long-term expenses in remedial programs, or to be proactive in influencing women and minorities to enter specific occupations. Whatever the reasons, if institutions enter these activities, not from a level of superiority but from a level of equal partnership with K–12 institutions, results can only be positive for the institutions. This report has been written to gain a better understanding of early intervention programs and to enter into this partnership with higher education's future students.

Jonathan D. Fife
Series Editor,
Professor of Higher Education Administration, and
Director, ERIC Clearinghouse on Higher Education

ACKNOWLEDGMENTS

The authors are grateful for expert assistance from Caryl DuBrock, Cristie Norwood, Betsy Sias, Kimberly Todd, and Eric Wibbing. All contributed their efforts as part of their responsibilities as graduate assistants in the higher education program at Arizona State University but, more than that, were active partners in the production of this publication. Carol Hanson and Donna Carroll provided much-needed technical assistance with an early draft of the manuscript. Special thanks are due to Jon Fife and Cherri Wright of the ERIC Clearinghouse staff as well as to two sets of anonymous reviewers who offered valuable critiques at crucial points of the manuscript's development. Caryl DuBrock deserves an extra measure of our gratitude for patiently and expertly accomplishing detailed work on the final version of the manuscript.

INTRODUCTION

The past two decades have witnessed an accelerating break-down of the historic separation of higher education from the elementary/secondary level. A vast, uncoordinated proliferation of programs has emerged to bridge the gap between the two levels by easing the transition of elementary and secondary students, especially those who are disadvantaged, into higher education. This report surveys government and private programs that aim to encourage the future college enrollment of elementary and secondary students, especially those from underrepresented groups, and the direct out-reach of collegiate academic programs to the lower schools for the same general purpose.

Opportunity for equal educational achievement and at-tainment for all citizens, regardless of race, sex, and socio-economic status, has been an important national goal since the mid-1960s. But in the late 1990s, socioeconomic status continues to be the main determinant of who goes to col-lege in all ability levels, and American Indians, African Americans, and Hispanics are underrepresented in attain-ment of high school diplomas and in participation in post-secondary education compared to whites and Asian Ameri-cans. Women now attain diplomas and degrees in numbers equal to men at all levels except the doctorate, and the gap there is narrowing rapidly. Women, however, still do not participate equally in the highest-paying and most presti-gious scientific fields (such as engineering) and professions. Instead, they continue to concentrate in the lower-paying "service" fields, such as nursing (rather than medicine or dentistry), social work, and education.

Failure of many groups in our society to participate equally is attributable to numerous complex and interrelated factors. It has been recognized that efforts to improve the chances of disadvantaged youth are best begun in the early grades. For example, preventing dropouts is a concern at all levels, but it is best pursued by not allowing academic achievement to lag too far behind in the critical primary grades. Retention is especially important, because attainment of at least a high school diploma is more and more often seen as vital for economic security in our increasingly tech-nological workplace. And one could argue, with the growing evidence that possession of a high school diploma is no longer sufficient for economic security, that a college degree may now be as necessary for economic security as a high school diploma was not long ago. To the extent this statement is true, preventing students from dropping out of high school is critical to individuals' economic success, and preventing college students from dropping out is becoming increasingly critical. Colleges and universities cannot be aloof from the need to prepare as many youth as possible to participate in higher education. Remedial programs for high school graduates who are not sufficiently prepared for college are expensive. Educators increasingly appreciate the need to address these problems through innovative coalitions of institutions of higher education and community schools.

Only in very recent decades has the idea of wide access to at least the first two years of college been seen as vital to full participation in the American Dream. The germinal ideas of this radical concept, unique to the United States, were expressed in the 1947 report of the Commission on Higher Education (the so-called Truman Commission) but did not come to fruition until the Kennedy and Johnson administrations. The Higher Education Act of 1965 initiated the major federal programs for student financial assistance that were to actualize the vision expressed by President Johnson at the ceremonial signing of the act: that this law "means that a high school senior anywhere in this great land of ours can apply to any college or university in any of the 50 states and not be turned away because his family is poor" (Committee on Education 1992, p. 3). The ensuing several years demonstrated to Congress, however, that grants given directly to institutions for the purpose of carrying out the national social justice agenda failed to overcome institutional self-interest and inertia. Therefore, it was not until the 1972 amendments to the act that the vision of universal access was expressed in legislation and appropriations. The key element was the Basic Educational Opportunity Grant program, which aimed to provide sufficient need-based gift aid to all students to attend the college of their choice. The grants (later renamed Pell grants) were sensitive to the cost of the college selected as well as to the ability of the student and his or her family to pay. Moreover, students' choice of eligible institutions was widened to include proprietary colleges offering vocational-technical (nonbaccalaureate) programs.

All of these federal efforts, especially the Pell grants, resulted in the most rapid increase in low-income and minority students' participation in higher education in our history.

This participation reached its peak in the late 1970s, when the availability of grants to attend college became well known in high schools. By the early 1980s, however, funding for grants and scholarships ("gift aid") failed to increase to meet students' financial need—and even lost ground to inflation through the decade. Meanwhile, college costs, especially tuition, increased rapidly. Emphasis in federal funding turned from gift aid to loans, with the result that these and other factors contributed to a decline in low-income and minority students' access to higher education. Those who do attend are increasingly concentrated in the lowest-cost institutions (the public two-year community colleges) or are successfully recruited by the less-than-two-year proprietary vocational-technical schools. And students who attend these proprietary vo-tech schools default at a high rate on the loans needed to meet the relatively high tuition. Default rates continue to be especially high among students who fail to complete their programs. Thus, the promise of universal access to higher education that seemed so attainable in the early 1970s remains unfulfilled by the late 1990s, although as a national goal, the promise remains viable. In early 1997, for example, the Clinton administration announced an initiative aimed at expanding access to at least the first two years of college.

To address these issues, this report first presents a brief review of the societal goals of equality for the nation's educational system. It then defines "early intervention" and "academic outreach" and synthesizes the demographic and educational problems and challenges related to the purposes of early intervention and academic outreach programs. It continues by describing several notable examples of private initiatives, such as the I Have A Dream program, presenting an overview of the burgeoning field of school-college collaborative efforts for early intervention and academic outreach, surveying and reviewing federal and state efforts, and discussing college and university academic outreach programs from several perspectives, including an overview of community colleges' involvement in school-college collaboration. The report concludes with evaluations of some early intervention programs and recommendations for follow-up by college and university administrators.

BACKGROUND

The United States has long been committed to higher levels of educational attainment for all its citizens than most other countries. This commitment began in the 19th century with the development of tuition-free, tax-supported elementary and secondary schools and then expanded into a system that required, by the middle of the 20th century, compulsory attendance through age 16. By 1950, the majority of 16- to 18 year-olds were attending high school with the intent to graduate, and increasing numbers of them were enrolled in postsecondary education, primarily in programs leading to the bachelor's degree.

But all groups did not share equally in the steep rise in educational attainment that occurred after World War II. Children in families of low socioeconomic status were especially likely to discontinue their schooling before completion of high school. At midcentury, higher education remained largely the province of middle- and higher-income families, although the 1944 GI Bill created an opportunity for greatly increased access to higher education for many who otherwise would not have been able to attend.

Equality of educational opportunity became an important social and economic agenda item for the country by the early 1960s. Research done in preparation for legal challenges to racial segregation in schools found great disparities in funding for, and quality of, schooling for racial minorities. Such inequity applied to lower socioeconomic groups of all races, and because racial minorities were disproportionally represented in lower socioeconomic classes, they were especially affected by lack of equal educational opportunity. Hence, such groups, especially African Americans who had been organized for political activism since early in the century, became special targets for improvement.

After racial segregation in schools was struck down in the landmark *Brown* v. *Board of Education* decision in 1954, attention turned toward studying the other factors related to differences in educational achievement and attainment. The findings of the prominent sociologist James S. Coleman were especially important in calling attention to family and neighborhood influences on educational achievement. Coleman maintained that while it was important to equalize school resources, attention must also be paid to differences existing among children at the beginning of schooling as well as at the end of schooling that could not be attributed to schooling alone. Specifically, he emphasized two important findings:

. . . (1) these minority children have a serious educational deficiency at the start of school, which is obviously not a result of school; and (2) they have an even more serious deficiency at the end of school, which is obviously in part a result of school (Coleman 1966, p. 72–73).

The nonschool part of the deficiency of minority children is pervasive:

Altogether, the sources of inequality of educational opportunity appear to lie first in the home itself and the cultural influences immediately surrounding the home; then they lie in the schools' ineffectiveness to free achievement from the impact of the home, and in the schools' homogeneity, which perpetuates the social influences of the home and its environs (pp. 73–74).

Coleman's final conclusions were reported in 1966, but his basic findings about the close relationship between poverty and achievement in school have stood the test of time. The 1995 edition of the congressionally mandated annual report *The Condition of Education* notes that:

. . . social scientists attribute much of the white-minority differences in achievement to the higher incidence of poverty in the families of minority children and the lower average educational levels of their parents. It is difficult for schools to compensate for such disadvantages (National Center 1995a, p. v).

Coleman's early findings in 1963 and 1964 were widely debated, but most observers believe they influenced the Great Society legislation of the mid-1960s, which includes the Civil Rights Act of 1964, the Elementary and Secondary Education Act (ESEA) of 1965, and the Higher Education Act (HEA) of 1965. These and other federal laws not only included efforts aimed at equalizing the resources of schools and the opportunity to attend them, but also sought to improve educational achievement and attainment by targeting a variety of support services to previously underrepresented groups. These services were intended to improve the achievement of minority children so that they not only would stay in school until high school graduation, but also be prepared for further education. In other words, the goal was to intervene by overcoming the negative influences of home and neighborhood that doomed many minority children to poor grades, dropping out of school early, and little hope of ever enrolling in college.

The HEA spawned a variety of federal programs, such as Talent Search, that aimed to encourage and recruit minority students to enroll in college and other programs that provided support after matriculation.

Early Intervention and Academic Outreach Defined

"Early intervention" is a generic concept that has been, and continues to be, applied to many different fields, including education. This report, however, focuses primarily on programs for school children that affect their persistence to high school graduation and enrollment in postsecondary education. In practice, most such programs target middle and high school students, although an increasing number focus on children in the early grades.

This report uses the definition stated in Title II of the 1992 reauthorization of the Higher Education Act as a unifying concept. According to the mission statement of the National Early Intervention Scholarship and Partnership Program authorized by Title II:

> *The Secretary [of Education] is authorized . . . to establish a program that (1) encourages States to provide or maintain a guarantee to eligible low-income students who obtain a high school diploma (or its equivalent), financial assistance necessary to permit them to attend an institution of higher education; and (2) provides incentives to States, in cooperation with local educational agencies, institutions of higher education, community organizations, and [businesses,] to provide (a) additional counseling, mentoring, academic support, outreach, and supportive services to elementary, middle, and secondary students who are at risk of dropping out of school; and (b) information for students and their parents about the advantages of obtaining a postsecondary education and their college financial options* (Higher Education Act of 1992, P.L. 102–325, 20 USC 1070a–21).

Nearly all the programs discussed in this report include at least one of the four main elements of this definition (financial assistance, collaboration among programs and agencies, support services, and information about college for students and parents), and most include at least two. This federal definition is highly useful for this report, because, even though it specifically defines a federal-state partnership, it is, like the wide array of public and private programs reviewed, comprehensive and multifaceted. It seems clear that the breadth of this federal definition was derived from a wide range of input and thus reflects the bewildering diversity of the early intervention activities reviewed in preparation for writing the law.

Many terms are similar in meaning to aspects of "early intervention" as defined above. For example, some state-funded programs use "early awareness" to indicate the goal of informing young children from underrepresented groups about the possibility of attending college. "Early eligibility" programs focus on informing at-risk children about the availability of student financial assistance for college and how they can be eligible for such funds. "Guaranteed-tuition programs" typically promise that funds to pay for college tuition and books will be available for at-risk children upon graduation from high school if they meet certain academic standards, such as an acceptable high school grade point average, or behavioral standards, such as avoidance of drugs and alcohol. These and other terms are, for the purpose of this report, considered to be included in the federal definition used as the unifying concept.

Academic outreach programs are closely related to, and interact with, early intervention programs sponsored by public and private agencies as defined previously. This report defines "academic outreach" as those programs that originate from the schools, colleges, and universities themselves. Thus, academic outreach is a special type of early intervention, and much of this report focuses on how colleges and universities reach out to encourage and assist school children to enroll in postsecondary education. While the concepts of early intervention and academic outreach overlap a great deal, differentiation between institutionally originated academic outreach and all other early intervention programs is useful to divide this extremely diverse field for purposes of this report.

Academic outreach programs can be divided into two general types. The first type of institutional academic outreach encourages at-risk students to plan for college with no focus on a particular academic discipline. The second type focuses on recruiting and preparing promising at-risk students for matriculation into specific academic disciplines offered by an institution. Academic outreach programs have two benefits: (1) They enhance educational opportunity in the institution's service area; and (2) they increase participation of at-risk students in specific disciplines within the institution as well as increase the institution's overall enrollment.

The second (academic outreach programs) type focuses on recruiting and preparing promising at-risk students for matriculation into specific academic disciplines offered by an institution.

Why Intervene?

This section outlines the basic elements of the particular problems addressed by early intervention. While the problems are generally familiar to the higher education community, they are reviewed here because of their direct relevance to the proliferation of early intervention programs. The problems and issues include demographic changes and the need to maintain wide access to postsecondary opportunity; high dropout rates, particularly of at-risk youth, before high school graduation; the negative effects on future employment and earnings of low educational attainment; low academic achievement and failure to complete high school courses that qualify students for admission to college; and the discouraging combination of rapidly rising costs of college and the continuing shortfall of financial aid to fill the gap for needy students.

Demographics

It is well known that the racial/ethnic distribution of the school-age population (5 to 17) is changing as the nation approaches the turn of the century; these changes are then projected to accelerate rapidly in the first half of the next century. The 1990 Census shows that slightly over two-thirds (68.6 percent) of school children are white (non-Hispanic). The next largest group is African Americans (15.1 percent), followed by Hispanics (11.8 percent) and much smaller percentages of Asian and Pacific Islanders (3.4 percent) and American Indians, Eskimos, and Aleuts (1.1 percent). This distribution will not change markedly by 2000 except that the white population will drop to 64.3 percent and the Hispanic percentage will increase to 14.5 percent; the remaining groups will gain no more than 1 percent. By the middle of the next century, however, the racial/ethnic profile of school children will change quite significantly. Whites will be in the minority (41.5 percent), and Hispanics will account for over one-fourth (26.9 percent). African Americans will account for nearly one-fifth (19.2 percent), and Asians and Pacific Islanders will have more than doubled in proportion, from 4.4 percent to 10.9 percent. American Indians, Eskimos, and Aleuts will remain a very small percentage, and their share will actually drop to 1.5 percent, from 1.8 percent at the beginning of the century (figures calculated from *Current Population Reports*, U.S. Bureau of the Census 1993).

What is important in this changing profile is the link between minority status and poverty, poverty being the most crucial factor putting children at risk for dropping out of school before completing high school. "The effects of poverty on children's education are well documented. Children from poor families have lower-than-average achievement and higher-than-average dropout rates" (National Center 1996a, p. 142). The link between poverty and minority status has long been established and is seemingly intractable. In 1960, before the War on Poverty, 65.6 percent of African-American children lived in poverty, compared to 20 percent of white children. By 1970, these figures had changed to 41.5 percent and 10.5 percent, respectively (National Center 1996a, p. 142). Between 1975 and 1994, however, racial differences among children in poverty were both persistent and pronounced. The percent of white children in poverty ranged from 12.5 percent to 17 percent, with an average of 15.3 percent over the 16-year period. The percent of African-American children in poverty ranged from 41.4 percent to 47.3 percent, with an overall average of 44.3 percent. Over the same 16-year period, the percent of Hispanic children in poverty ranged from 33 percent to 41.1 percent, with an overall average of 37.7 percent (figures calculated from *Current Population Reports*, U.S. Bureau of the Census 1994).

Poverty status in these figures refers to annual income, but perhaps an even more telling statistic is the difference in disposable assets. In terms of supporting the college enrollment and persistence of children, a family's liquid finances and other assets that can be used for collateral (real estate that can be mortgaged, automobiles, annuities and other investments, for example) are very significant. And the difference between whites and minority groups in this regard is very striking. For example, the average net worth of such assets for white households in 1988 was $43,280, more than *10* times that for African-American households ($4,170) and nearly *eight* times that for Hispanic households ($5,520) (U.S. Bureau of the Census 1988).

These differences in assets persist throughout the life span. For example, a recent national survey of adults aged 51 to 61 by the Rand Corporation reveals that "race differences in wealth are enormous, far outdistancing racial income differences. For every dollar of wealth a middle-aged white household has, an African-American household has 27 cents" (J. Smith 1995, p. 167). These figures refer to net worth, a combination of assets from all sources, including real estate, vehicles, stocks, and bonds. Older adult African Americans and Hispanics are at a particular disadvantage in investments that could be used to assist children or grandchildren with college costs. "The minority deficit is especially large concerning those financial assets with a long-term investment component, where the white advantage is tenfold in stocks and thirtyfold in bonds" (p. 168). Further, the disparity in liquid financial assets that are already or can be quickly converted to ready cash is enormous. Whereas the median financial assets of households headed by a white person aged 51 to 61 are $17,300,

> . . . *[those] of the average black or Hispanic household are stunningly low. . . . Summed across all forms of financial wealth, the median black household has only $400; the median Hispanic household fares even worse with only $78. For all practical purposes, the average middle-aged black or Hispanic household has no liquid assets at [its] disposal* (J. Smith 1995, pp. 167–68).

The figures can be somewhat misleading, because poverty is not as persistent for some groups as others. Dollar figures reflecting poverty status can change from year to year for any given household. For example, the vast majority of students in doctoral and professional programs are white, and those with school-age children often qualify for poverty status. But for most such children, this status is temporary and will change toward the other end of the family income distribution range soon after their parents' graduation. For many poor minority children, on the other hand, the condition is persistent and generates important qualitative differences that bode ill for their educational attainment.

These qualitative differences were reported in a massive 1986 assessment of federal support services for children that originated as Chapter 1 of the 1965 ESEA (changed in 1981 to authorization under the Educational Consolidation and Improvement Act). Chapter 1 has been and continues to be the main federal title that appropriates funds to help the educational chances of children in low-income families. Beginning as it did during the Great Society's War on Poverty, its premise was (and is) that poverty and low achievement in school are related. Consequently, funds are allocated according to the number of poor children who reside in a specific school district. A remarkable finding of the assessment is that, while an individual child's achievement in school and his or her family's poverty status were associated, the association was not very strong; that is, many poor children did well in school, and many low achievers were not from poor families.

On the other hand, when looking at schools *rather than individual children within the schools, the association was much stronger: Schools with large proportions of poor students were far more likely to exhibit lower average achievement scores than other schools* (Kennedy, Jung, and Orland 1986, pp. 3–4).

The implications of this finding are that schools in "dense pockets" of poverty are so educationally inadequate they drag down the achievement of both poor and nonpoor children; conversely, poor children in non-poverty-impacted schools will do better than they would have done in schools swamped with pupils of poverty status. This finding is logical, considering that other research has shown that "poverty-impacted" schools are usually deficient in such resources as experienced, expert teachers and modern equipment. As mentioned earlier, Coleman and others have found that attention must also be paid to the negative influences of family and neighborhood on educational achievement. Many of the early intervention programs described in this report have the goal of increasing the self-esteem of students from disadvantaged educational settings.

Attention and concern continue to focus on minorities because, as indicated by the census figures cited earlier, minority children are much more likely to be poor. Further, their poverty has a qualitative aspect with regard to measures of its intensity and persistence: "Children who experience long-term family poverty and children who live in areas with high concentrations of poverty are more likely to belong to minority groups" (Kennedy, Jung, and Orland 1986, p. 7). Specifically, among children in grades seven and eight, an age when plans for staying in or leaving school are beginning to form, only 9.2 percent of white children are counted as poor, compared to 38.5 percent of African Americans and 33.7 percent of Hispanics (p. 34).

In terms of the persistence of poverty, a study done by the University of Michigan Institute for Social Research found that "the average nonblack child is expected to spend eight-tenths of a year in poverty during his or her 15 years of childhood. The average black child is expected to spend 5.4 years in poverty during this period" (Duncan and Rogers 1985, p. 46). This finding probably understates the specific comparison between white and African-American children because "nonblack" includes Hispanics and American Indians with high rates of poverty.

The focus on minorities because of their relatively high poverty rates should not obscure the fact that very many white children also live in poverty and also are at risk to fail in the educational system. For example, the Chapter 1 assessment report points out that researchers' findings:

> . . . contradict the common belief that the program serves primarily black students. For every 100 black students served by the program, there are more than 150 white students served. This discrepancy occurs in part because, even though white students have a lower poverty rate than blacks, there are so many more white students altogether that they are likely to constitute the majority of any group—rich or poor, old or young (Kennedy, Jung, and Orland 1986, p. 73).

Dropouts and educational attainment
Most early intervention programs focus on at-risk youth, especially those from low-income ethnic or minority families. In this report, "at risk" refers to students with a higher-

than-average likelihood of dropping out before completion of high school or, for those who finish with their age cohort, significantly less likelihood of pursuing postsecondary education. Recent research on the database from the National Educational Longitudinal Study of 1988 (NELS:88) points to six characteristics of eighth graders identified as at-risk students: They (1) live in single-parent families, (2) have family incomes of less than $15,000 annually, (3) have an older sibling who has dropped out, (4) have parents who did not finish high school, (5) have limited proficiency in English, or (6) are at home without adult supervision for more than three hours a day. The researchers found that students with two or more of these risk factors are more likely than those with no risk factors to have low grades and perform poorly on a standardized test measuring eighth grade achievement (Green and Scott 1995, p. 2). Discontinuing one's education before at least finishing high school not only generally results in lack of postsecondary education, but also is related strongly to unemployment, low income with little likelihood of improvement, and placement on the welfare rolls. Further, the continuing rise in technical and literacy requirements for entry-level employment, as reflected in higher and higher levels of educational credentials used as "screening" elements for consideration of job applicants, leaves dropouts farther and farther behind.

Dropouts, particularly among the low-income/minority cohorts projected to grow rapidly in coming decades, remain one of the country's most serious and persistent problems. A symposium convened by the American Council on Education (ACE) and the National Association of Student Financial Aid Administrators (NASFAA) underscored the magnitude and gravity of the problem:

> As a result of these sweeping demographic changes, the high percentages of school dropouts—already about half of students entering ninth grade in urban areas—are likely to increase. Unless there are serious, comprehensive, coordinated interventions at early stages in the lives of at-risk students, a significant percentage of the class of 2001 will be alienated from school by sixth grade and on the street by age 16. Many will . . . not work, pay taxes, vote, or concern themselves with others, but instead drain resources. A significant number of

these individuals may find community (and commerce) in gangs that require society to provide more police, wardens, and jails, or they may become homeless and require public shelter and assistance. Henry Levin of Stanford University estimated several years ago that the cost of school dropouts, current ages 25 to 34, amounted conservatively to $77 billion every year: $71 billion in lost tax revenues, $3 billion for welfare and unemployment, and $3 billion for crime prevention. Educators note that it costs states more to keep an individual in prison for one year than it costs to pay for four years of college (National Association 1989, pp. 1–2).

The figures that compare the societal benefits of a well-educated citizenry with the staggering costs of a poorly educated one take on added urgency when the sheer numbers of potential dropouts are considered. For example, it is well established that poverty status is one of the factors most strongly related to dropping out (National Center 1996a, pp. 48–49). More than one-fifth of the nation's school children are poor (22 percent or 14.6 million) and live in neighborhoods and attend schools together (National Center 1995b, p. xi). The relationship between socioeconomic status and educational attainment is not only strong but also persistent. The High School and Beyond (HSB) longitudinal study found that, of the high school sophomores in 1980, only 1.4 percent from the highest socioeconomic quartile failed to graduate but that 9 percent of this cohort from the lowest socioeconomic quartile had not earned a high school diploma 12 years later. Given the correlation between socioeconomic status and minority status, completion of high school would be expected to vary among racial and ethnic groups. The HSB data show that, while 4.9 percent of white sophomores failed to graduate, more than double that percentage (11.9) of Hispanics and more than triple that percentage (17.8) of American Indians also failed to graduate. Comparable figures were 6.9 percent for African Americans and 0.6 percent for Asian/Pacific Islanders (National Center 1995b, p. 311). The "success story" of the 1980 sophomores who attained at least a bachelor's degree by 1992 also showed strong correlations with socioeconomic status and race/ethnicity: Only 6.4 percent of the students from the lowest socioeconomic quartile earned a bachelor's degree, compared with 19 percent of the students from families in the middle socioeconomic group and 41.2 percent of those in the highest socioeconomic quartile. The percentages of those earning at least a bachelor's degree also varied widely among racial and ethnic groups: whites, 23.1 percent; African Americans, 10 percent; Hispanics, 9 percent; Asian/Pacific Islanders, 32.7 percent, and American Indian/Alaskan Native, 6.7 percent.

Employment and welfare status

Low educational attainment is strongly related to rate of unemployment. The 1993 overall unemployment rate for adults was 4.8 percent; that rate doubled (9.8 percent) for adults without a high school diploma but was only 2.6 percent for those with at least a bachelor's degree (U.S. Dept. of Labor 1994). According to data from the March 1992 Current Population Surveys, dropouts are not only more likely to be unemployed, they are also much more likely to be on welfare. "In 1992, high school dropouts were three times more likely to receive income from AFDC [Aid to Families with Dependent Children] or public assistance than high school graduates who did not go on to college (17 percent versus 6 percent)" (National Center 1995a, p. 96). In contrast, college graduates are very rarely on welfare: From 1972 through 1992, the rate was always below 1 percent for persons with at least a bachelor's degree (p. 96).

The relationship between welfare status and participation in postsecondary education is important, because the welfare system is targeted toward single mothers and their dependents. About 90 percent of the current welfare population receives welfare funds under AFDC. "The system was designed after World War II to support single mothers who lost husbands during the war and has continued to provide financial assistance primarily to single women and their children" (Institute 1995, p. 1). The shift in purpose from temporary assistance for young war widows to quasi-permanent status for women who have little likelihood of entering the workforce, however, has greatly affected the educational attainment of the children in these families. One anomaly of the AFDC regulations in the 1970s and most of the 1980s was that efforts by AFDC mothers to enter postsecondary educational programs could result in the loss of welfare support. Many women on AFDC who applied for and received financial aid to attend college found that the grants for tuition and books were counted as income. And the increase in income was often sufficient to raise them above the ceiling for eligibility for welfare support. For nearly all such women, this Catch-22 meant they were blocked from attempts to break the cycle of poverty through postsecondary education. The federal Family Support Act in 1988 attempted to alleviate this problem through the Job Opportunities Basic Skills (JOBS) program.

> *The concept behind the JOBS program has been generally supported because it allows the government to provide to families and, at the same time, to encourage work and financial independence. However, since implementation costs are high and budgets are tight, states enroll only a small percent of the welfare recipients eligible to receive training through the JOBS program. Many individuals who wish to participate in the program are prevented from doing so because of state budgetary limitations. Instead, they continue to receive AFDC, even though access to training would enable them to become self-sufficient and leave the program* (Institute 1995, p. 2).

Recent congressional budget reforms will have the effect of greatly reducing, if not eliminating, the already small number of women receiving AFDC who benefit from participating in the postsecondary portion of the JOBS program (p. 10). The Clinton administration followed earlier congressional initiatives by proposing a "welfare-to-work" tax credit in spring 1997. The proposed tax credit imposes draconian measures to move welfare recipients off AFDC and other programs.

In contrast to the high rates of unemployment and welfare status of high school dropouts, participation in postsecondary education reaps great societal and individual benefits from much higher average annual income. A strong correlation has always existed between annual income and educational attainment. The continuing redistribution of job-related income according to technical literacy and educational credentials indicates that the correlation continues to strengthen. The difference in annual income between men who failed to complete high school and those with at least four years of college grew markedly from 1970 to 1990. In 1970, male dropouts earned an average of $8,514 per year, compared to

$13,264 for college graduates; in 1980, these figures were $16,101 and $24,311, respectively. By 1990, the average college graduate's annual income ($39,238) was nearly double the dropout's ($20,902). Type of occupation and opportunity for advancement are also correlated with educational credentials. In particular, a bachelor's degree often qualifies the recipient for a high-level position. For example, a survey of recent college graduates shows that about three-fourths (73 percent) were employed in managerial, professional, and technical areas within one year of their graduation in spring 1990 (National Center 1995b, p. 404). Conversely, "only 61 percent of 1993–94 [high school] dropouts were in the labor force (employed or looking for work), and 30 percent of them were unemployed" (p. 409).

These figures show high employment rates, income, and occupational status for college graduates, contrasted with the strong likelihood for dropouts to be unemployed or on welfare or, even if employed, to be in low-income jobs with little chance for advancement or even job stability. Given these contrasts, the findings of surveys of high school students showing the increasingly and perhaps overly optimistic expectations for a college education and high-paying, prestigious occupations are quite poignant. More than nine of every 10 (91.4 percent) of 1993 high school seniors planned to go to college, compared with 69.3 percent of seniors 10 years earlier. Moreover, these rosy expectations in 1993 ranged across all racial and ethnic, socioeconomic status, and even test performance categories. Even within the racial/ethnic group with the lowest-ranking expectation (American Indians), 86.5 percent expected to go to college, as did over three-fourths (77.8 percent) of seniors in the lowest test performance quartile and over four-fifths (82.6 percent) of seniors in the lowest socioeconomic quartile (National Center 1995b, p. 137). The glowing expectations of high school seniors extend to occupational plans. About seven out of 10 (69.7 percent) of the 1992 high school seniors expected to be in professional, managerial, or technical occupations, with these lofty plans generally extending across all racial/ethnic groups and socioeconomic quartiles (p. 135).

Academic achievement and courses taken
Offsetting the rising expectations of at-risk youth for postsecondary education and high-paying, prestigious occupa-

tions is their continuing poor achievement in critical subjects and failure to take high school courses required for admission to college.

The National Assessment of Educational Progress (NAEP) project has tracked the achievement levels of a sample of American school children at ages 9, 13, and 17. The project also gathers data on socioeconomic status along with the scores on tests it administers to a national sample. NAEP has gathered comparative test scores on reading, math, and science since the 1970s. More recently, NELS:88 began tracking grades and educational attainment of eighth graders, beginning in 1988. These two databases provide much of the current insight into progress and problems of school children as they complete K–12 education and move into postsecondary education. Because of the interrelation between minority status and risk factors, these studies have paid much attention to the educational achievement of minorities. The findings thus far are not encouraging.

> *Another area of continuing concern is the academic achievement of minority students in elementary and secondary school. For example, in 1992, the average reading proficiency scores of black 17-year-olds were . . . similar to the average proficiency scores of white 13-year-olds. The white-Hispanic reading gap at age 17 was a little narrower. White-black and white-Hispanic proficiency score differences were of similar magnitudes in science, although they were smaller in mathematics. It is also worrisome that despite a narrowing in the white-minority gap in achievement during the 1980s, particularly in mathematics, recent data [raise] the possibility that the gap is no longer closing* (National Center 1995b, p. v).

The *Condition of Education* report in 1994 focused on African-American students, while the 1995 report focused on Hispanic students. The earlier study found that "gaps in the academic performance of black and white students appear as early as age 9 and persist through age 17" (T. Smith 1995a, p. 3). The gaps exist in reading, mathematics, and science subjects, all of which are important to success in postsecondary education. The gaps at age 13, as students enter high school, are problematic, because tracking into

Concern
about the
continuing
differences
is urgent
because
Hispanics
are by far
the fastest-
growing
ethnic
group in the
school pop-
ulation. The
differences
begin early
and persist
through the
educational
pipeline . . .

college preparatory courses is often based on performance in prior grades. The persistence of the gap at age 17, as students near high school graduation, is cause for additional concern. Not only has the gap increased to the extent that African-American 17-year-olds are reading at a level of proficiency about the same as white 13-year-olds; this gap exists even after a much larger percentage of African-American students have dropped out. NELS:88 and other data show that dropouts tend to be much lower achievers than persisters (T. Smith 1995a, p. 4).

Studies focusing on Hispanic students have shown that students of this minority status have made "important educational gains over the past two decades. . . . [Nevertheless,] Hispanics trail their white counterparts with respect to educational access, achievement, and attainment, although some of these differences have narrowed over time" (T. Smith 1995b, p. 1). Concern about the continuing differences is urgent because Hispanics are by far the fastest-growing ethnic group in the school population. The differences begin early and persist through the educational pipeline, including very high Hispanic dropout rates in high school. For example, Hispanic children have far less preschool experience: Only 17 percent of them begin kindergarten with some preschool experience, compared to 38 percent of white kindergartners (p. 2). As with African Americans, academic achievement gaps between Hispanic and white children begin as early as age 9 and persist through age 17, although the gaps are not as large as between African Americans and whites. The smaller comparative gaps by age 17, however, must be interpreted in the light of much greater high school dropout rates for Hispanics than either African Americans or whites. The same studies that have shown racial/ethnic differences in academic achievement also show similar differences between high socioeconomic and low socioeconomic status for students that cut across racial/ethnic categories.

Many states have increased the number of courses required for high school graduation, especially in English, math, science, foreign languages, and computer literacy. These changes have been made partly to respond to criticisms of K–12 education, beginning with *A Nation at Risk* in 1983, and partly to accommodate higher education institutions' desiring students who are better prepared. Over 40 states imposed increased course requirements for graduation between 1988 and 1991 (National Center 1996b, pp. 144–48). Many educators have been concerned that the increased requirements for all schools will adversely affect low-income/ minority students in the schools of low educational quality they typically attend. The findings of a Rand research center study (Oakes 1990) seem to bear out the concerns. The study examined the distribution of science and mathematics learning opportunities in elementary and secondary schools and found that low-income/minority inner-city students have relatively fewer opportunities to benefit from science and mathematics courses. These students have considerably fewer materials, less-qualified teachers, and lower-quality learning activities. These findings apply to entire schools as well as to individual classrooms.

Given that low-income/minority children have fewer school resources to help them meet increased high school graduation standards, it is not surprising that they do poorly compared to high-income/majority children. Analysis of the NELS:88 data found that, while no significant difference exists by gender in taking academic courses, students from high socioeconomic status complete more of these courses, and that "among students with comparable [socioeconomic status], the differences in the number of courses completed between whites, blacks, and Hispanics are insignificant" (Hoffer, Rasinski, and Moore 1995, p. 2). Asian-American students complete more math and science courses within all socioeconomic categories than other groups. Students who complete the increased course requirements for math and science "show greater achievement score gains during high school, regardless of gender, race/ethnicity, and socioeconomic class" (p. 2). Of course, offsetting this relative equality in taking courses and achievement among students meeting the increased requirements is the continuing disparity between such students and at-risk students who more often do not attempt such advanced courses or perform poorly in them when they do. For example, 65 percent of at-risk students "failed to complete a basic sequence of high school courses, compared to 37 percent of those with no risk factors" (Green and Scott 1995, p. 1). As would be expected from these findings, students of low socioeconomic status show significantly lower achievement in reading, math, and science; this gap would be expected from the lower rate of taking courses in these subjects.

Thus, at-risk high school students, even if they persist to graduation, tend to be less prepared for college than other students, both in terms of meeting increasingly stringent course requirements and achievement levels in academic subject areas.

Student financial aid and college costs

Added to the factors of poverty, broken families, low academic achievement, and others that hamper the outlook of at-risk children are the daunting financial aspects of postsecondary education. Simply put, the costs of college keep rising faster than the financial resources of most families, and the student financial aid programs intended to fill this growing gap have failed to keep pace (College Board 1995). In February 1992, the principal congressional committee preparing for the reauthorization of the HEA warned that "the gap between family resources and college costs is steadily widening, and the ability of the federal student financial assistance programs to fill that gap and enable students to pursue education beyond high school is also steadily eroding" (Committee on Education and Labor 1992, p. 3). When the reauthorization became law in August 1992, it not only continued but also accelerated the shift in federal financial assistance from gift aid (grants and scholarships) to loans. The original HEA and its reauthorizing amendments through 1976 emphasized gift aid and saw loans as supplemental. In particular, Pell grants, authorized in the 1972 amendments as Basic Educational Opportunity Grants, were to provide a "floor" of gift aid that was sensitive to the cost of each college and thus provide not only access but a reasonable measure of choice to all youth considering college. These need-based grants, along with other types of aid, aimed at destroying the economic barriers that blocked low-income/minority families from sending their children to college. The total amount of Pell grants awarded after passage of the 1972 amendments leaped from $159 million in 1973–74 to nearly $3.75 billion in 1976–77, surpassing the total amount of guaranteed loans awarded by $376 million (College Board 1995, p. 13). In the mid-1970s, annual college costs had not yet begun to increase rapidly, and maximum Pell grants as a share of total cost of attendance reached their zenith, covering nearly 80 percent of the costs of public four-year colleges and nearly 40 percent of the costs of private colleges in 1975–76. A precipitous decline in the share began in 1979–80, however, and by 1994–95 the share of the cost of attendance covered by the Pell grant maximum dropped to about one-third in public four-year institutions and about 10 percent in private ones (College Board 1995, p. 3).

Meanwhile, over this same general period, the cost of college attendance rose much more rapidly than family income and available gift aid. Average tuition and fees, measured in constant 1994 dollars, rose 38.4 percent for private four-year colleges and 56.8 percent for public four-year colleges from 1985–86 to 1993–94 (College Board 1995, p. 6). Median family income increased only 10 percent during that period. As detrimental to college access as these trends were, the last half of this period witnessed an increasingly severe erosion of the ability of families to pay college costs. The average cost of attendance at private four-year colleges rose 60 percent from 1980–81 to 1992–93, that for public four-year colleges 44 percent, while the recession of the 1980s held median family income in constant dollars to only a 3 percent increase over this same period. In constant 1992 dollars, the costs of an average private college rose from $9,069 to $14,514, those in the public sector from $4,134 to $5,936, while annual family income grew by only about $1,000, from $35,839 to $36,812 (College Board 1995).

These trends do not belie the fact that the federal government has appropriated massive sums for student financial aid. It provided nearly $200 billion for need-based aid in the 1980s alone (National Commission 1993). Current federal expenditures are high: The preliminary estimate for 1994–95 is over $35 billion. The federal government is the major source of financial aid, providing about 75 percent of the total, while institutional and private sources provide about 19 percent and state-provided aid accounts for about 6 percent. The overall total for 1994–95 is $48.8 billion, a huge sum by any measure (College Board 1995).

Although large sums are being provided, the continuing twofold problem of student aid is that college costs have risen more rapidly than aid awarded and the type of aid has shifted increasingly from gift aid to loans. This dual problem has particular impact on low-income/minority students, as reflected in the fact that socioeconomic status is still the major determinant of attending college within all ability levels

(Mortenson 1990). The rapid rise in costs, particularly in the public and private four-year sectors, has relegated most low-income students to the lowest-cost sector, public two-year community colleges. The existence of this sector has maintained access for low-income/minority students, but this sector of higher education has, over the last 20 years, successfully transferred only small percentages of its students to the four-year colleges for completion of baccalaureate degrees.

Two aspects of the shift from gift aid to loans impact heavily on low-income/minority students. First, these students are more likely to default on their loans. Defaulters tend to come from low-income family backgrounds, and they disproportionately belong to racial minorities. Default is relatively more frequent in community colleges and proprietary institutions (Schwartz and Baum 1989). And defaulters are in double jeopardy, because they typically drop out early in their college careers (usually in their first academic term) and thus have loans to repay but do not have the training, educational credentials, or higher level of income that completing their programs would have provided. Even those students who complete their programs often graduate and attempt to begin their careers saddled with large loans accumulated over the entire program.

The second problem related to the impact of loans on low-income/minority students is the presumed reluctance of such students to accumulate debt as a means to obtain a credential that is a number of years in the future (the national average time to a baccalaureate degree is now over five years). Definitive research on the willingness or reluctance of low-income/minority students to borrow has yet to be conducted, but what is known is that students from poor families, unlike those from middle- and high-income families, do not have the family assets that can be converted to cash for college. Moreover, they can rarely afford the luxury of loss of personal income during the five or more years of a baccalaureate program. In many cases, students from poor families may well be expected to work as soon as legally possible to help support their parents, siblings, and perhaps other relatives as well; one study found that such expectations often occurred among high school valedictorians from low-income families (Arnold 1995, pp. 137, 140, 148). Overall, the Great Society's goal of banishing economic bar-

The rapid rise in costs, particularly in the public and private four-year sectors, has relegated most low-income students to the lowest-cost sector, public two-year community colleges.

riers to college enrollment has not been accomplished by the student financial system, and universal access has remained a "dream denied" (Fenske and Gregory 1994). Further, even the limited gains in access and retention produced by student financial aid are in danger of being reduced, as the large annual appropriations and problems of default made student aid a target for cutbacks in the fiscally conservative Congress elected in fall 1994. As of February 1996, it was "expected that federal funding for student aid [would] be significantly reduced with the initiative to balance the budget within seven years" (Long 1996, p. 6).

In response to the continuing fiscal conservatism of Congress through 1996 and into 1997, the Clinton administration took a bold departure from the usual strategy of struggling with Congress to increase appropriations for student aid. In August 1996, the Clinton administration announced five tax proposals that, if enacted, would provide nearly $40 billion to pay for attending college. The following year, the president and Congress reached agreement on these proposals as part of the legislation aimed at balancing the budgets. Thirty-one billion dollars of the 1997 mandated tax breaks are to be realized in the form of annual tuition credits. Using the tax code to support higher education had last been used as a major proposal during the Carter administration in the late 1970s. President Clinton's initiatives were quickly criticized as failing to benefit low-income students (Gladieux and Reischauer 1996), with the critics suggesting what they believed to be a more viable alternative to tuition credits: "Investing in Pell grants is a more effective way to help both low- and moderate-income families and students get access to college" (Lederman 1997, p.A28). Although the initiatives also proposed a significant increase in Pell grants, observers gave this budget-based proposal little chance in the face of Congress's desire to achieve a balanced budget (Burd and Haworth 1997). The overall prospect in late spring 1997 was that the tax code proposals had a much better chance of approval by Congress than the budget proposals. The result was little optimism for increased access to college for low-income youth.

PRIVATE INITIATIVES

Changes in tax laws concerning contributions for charitable purposes over the past two decades may have adversely affected the number of nonpublic early intervention programs started and/or continued. It also seems likely that the establishment of federal and state programs described in this report decreased the interest and willingness of individuals, corporations, and foundations to support private initiatives. Because private and public initiatives each affect the other sector, it would be highly useful to have a survey of all types of programs currently existing, an undertaking beyond the scope of this report.

Foundation awards related to early intervention listed in *Chronicle of Higher Education* from January 1995 through February 1996 were reviewed, however. Fifteen grants totaling over $3.5 million were awarded for a wide range of early intervention programs by the Ford Foundation, the Houston Endowment, the Kellogg Foundation, the Carnegie Corporation, and others. Grants were awarded to public and private two-year and four-year colleges, to school districts, and to higher education associations. One particularly active foundation in this area is the DeWitt Wallace–*Reader's Digest* Fund. Under its School-to-College program, the fund has provided more than $7 million to projects that offer financial assistance, mentoring, counseling, and academic preparation for low-income youth. An additional $8.2 million since 1991 has supported projects under its School/Family Partnership program, which seeks to increase involvement of minority or low-income parents in their children's education (DeWitt Wallace 1996, pp. 33–34). The John S. and James L. Knight Foundation also has supported many projects emphasizing school-to-college collaboration.

This section reviews five examples of private initiatives aimed at early intervention. The examples, although only five in number, exhibit a wide range of scopes and missions. One was begun in 1963; the others are much more recent. Four are national in scope, but one sharply contrasting example targets 26 students who were classmates in a single elementary school classroom. Two programs work with a cross-section of at-risk pupils, two target academically talented youth, and one focuses on a particular minority group's participation in specialized academic disciplines.

The I Have A Dream Foundation

The I Have A Dream (IHAD) initiative, which "began quite by accident" is "perhaps today's most talked-about program for increasing college access for the poor," (Levine and Nidiffer 1996, p. 169). In 1981, Eugene Lang, a self-made millionaire, returned to P.S. 121, the elementary school he had attended more than 50 years earlier in East Harlem. When Lang was told that 75 percent of the sixth grade students to whom he spoke would never graduate from high school and that those who did graduate would not be adequately prepared for college, he made a spontaneous promise to these students. He promised all 61 students in the class full-tuition scholarships to college if they successfully graduated from high school. Further, he hired a social worker to help the children stay in school and provided additional academic support for those students requiring assistance. As a result, 90 percent of the class graduated from high school or received their GED certificates, and 60 percent went on to higher education, mostly at public four-year or community colleges.

Since 1981, the philanthropic gesture of Eugene Lang has grown into the I Have A Dream program, which now consists of over 160 IHAD projects in 27 states and 59 cities and involves over 12,000 students. A recent survey of 24 IHAD projects found that, in 1993, over 750 "dreamers" (as student participants are called) graduated from high school and more than 80 percent went on to college or vocational school.*
The IHAD projects provide individual support and guidance to disadvantaged children from elementary school through high school. It provides money to those students who graduate from high school to fill the gap between available scholarship assistance and the cost of tuition at a state college or university, and ongoing academic support, cultural and recreational activities, caring intervention, and personal guidance.

Each dreamer is encouraged to stay in school, with the hope that he or she will graduate from high school as a functionally literate student having an assured opportunity for higher education and/or fulfilling employment. Parents' involvement in IHAD projects is crucial, for the opportunities and experiences IHAD offers are most effective when parents encourage their children's participation. Dreamers' parents are expected to serve as mentors, activity leaders, and chaperons.

—
* IHAD brochure. 1994. New York, New York.

Project "sponsors" (individuals, corporations, or civic organizations) develop a personal commitment to the students through monetary and personal support. A sponsor typically "adopts" an entire elementary school grade, usually third grade, and provides or secures commitments of at least $400,000 for basic funding. Many sponsors raise such funds from other individuals, corporations, civic groups, and events.

IHAD policy urges the start of projects as early as funding permits but no later than graduation from elementary school. Most projects begin at third or fourth grade, and some are now beginning as early as second grade. The goal is eventually to begin all projects in kindergarten.

The I Have A Dream Foundation was established in 1986 in New York City to promote the program's growth and development, to determine program policies, to monitor the nationwide network of operating projects, to provide support and information services, and to extend community outreach. IHAD's original policy was focused on elementary schools for the projects, but the IHAD Foundation and the Department of Housing and Urban Development agreed to collaborate in 1992 and expand the program to establish projects in inner-city housing developments in association with community interest groups. Organizers assume that, by operating where the dreamers live, both students and parents will increase their participation in IHAD projects. Moreover, the public housing community can provide greater opportunities to develop convenient facilities to carry out academic, social, and recreational activities. It is highly recommended that a local college or university be associated as an affiliate sponsor with each project to provide an inspirational higher education presence, student and faculty resources, and the use of the physical facilities. Currently, six housing-based projects are in operation, and four more are being developed.

IHAD has directed special efforts to make colleges and universities effectively a part of a project's "life" by having them serve as sponsor affiliates. While this goal has not yet been achieved, colleges and universities have provided many resources and opportunities that should not go unnoted. As of February 1994, 72 private colleges and universities had given the IHAD Foundation written guarantees that any dreamer who applies for admission and is admitted will receive full financial aid based on need. Many colleges have undertaken to domicile local IHAD projects. They provide, among other things, office and activity space, guidance, and athletic and social facilities for the program's use. Many colleges and universities provide local IHAD projects and services, such as summer programs, tutoring, computer learning facilities, campus visits and activities, athletic facilities, program preparation, college preparatory aid, and mentoring relationships. Grinnell College in Iowa and Stanford University in California are the first institutions to take full responsibility for funding, providing for sponsorship and developing program and support services for IHAD projects. Yale University is organizing a similar project in New Haven, Connecticut, and the foundation is consulting with other colleges and universities considering IHAD projects.

And IHAD has spawned a number of public programs. The exact number is not known, but both Arizona's ASPIRE and New York's Liberty Scholarship and Partnership Program are modeled directly after IHAD.

A Better Chance

A Better Chance was founded in 1963 by representatives of 23 independent schools at Phillips Academy in Andover, Massachusetts, to consider ways and means of helping minority high school students who, because of lack of resources or cultural advantages, would be hampered in their ambitions to enter college. Headquartered in Boston, A Better Chance's mission has rested in a single goal: to substantially increase the number of well-educated people of color able to assume positions of leadership and responsibility in American society.*

Through its largest program, the College Preparatory Schools Program, A Better Chance identifies, recruits, selects, and places academically talented and motivated students of color in academically rigorous private and public high schools throughout the nation. More than 99 percent of A Better Chance's students go on to higher education, many at America's most selective colleges and universities. Nine out of 10 of them receive college degrees, and many go on to pursue graduate study.

A Better Chance has changed emphasis significantly over its more than 30-year history (Levine and Nidiffer 1996). The

---

* "Overview"—A Better Chance brochure. 1995. Boston, Massachusetts.

program boomed during its first decade. Between 1965 and 1969, for example, it garnered more than $5 million from the same federal program that was also supporting Upward Bound and received impressive support from foundations as well (pp. 164–65). Today, A Better Chance has a lower funding base, mainly from corporations, and "has had to dramatically reduce its program and cut back on recruitment and scholarships for low-income students" (p. 165). Further, the program "has shifted away from the poor and moved toward middle-class black students," specifically, toward those with high academic achievement and promise (p. 165).

In fall 1995, A Better Chance placed 334 promising minority youth in ABC member schools nationwide, bringing total enrollment of A Better Chance students to 1,146. Students come from 32 different states and attend schools in 27 states. A Better Chance has 178 member schools, representing some of the finest academic resources and facilities in the country. A Better Chance has an annual average of 57 affiliated colleges and universities, which help disseminate information to the students about their respective institutions and about application to college. In over three decades, A Better Chance has produced more than 8,000 alumni, most of whom have embarked on successful careers.

By concentrating its efforts on mathematics, EQUITY 2000 hopes to facilitate the completion of "gatekeeper" courses, that is, algebra and geometry, by the ninth and tenth grades, respectively.

EQUITY 2000

EQUITY 2000, an educational initiative of the College Board, aims to enhance minorities' preparation for higher education by offering academic outreach in mathematics to elementary, middle school, and secondary school students. The program has received funding over its eight-year history from many private foundations, including Carnegie, Ford, and Rockefeller, as well as the National Science Foundation. By concentrating its efforts on mathematics, EQUITY 2000 hopes to facilitate the completion of "gatekeeper" courses, that is, algebra and geometry, by the ninth and tenth grades, respectively. With these courses under their belts, participating students are prepared for, and have access to, demanding college preparatory curricula.*

Mathematics teachers, guidance counselors, and principals are trained to raise students' expectations, increase their motivation, and bolster academic preparation in middle and

---

* "EQUITY 2000: Academic Excellence for All Students." 1994. New York, New York.

high schools (College Board 1994b). Additional parties involved in the development of students include local site coordinators, superintendents of schools, community businesses, civic leaders, and parents. By incorporating a wide array of interested parties in its plan of action, EQUITY 2000 fosters comprehensive, potentially permanent, district-wide reform rather than isolated cases of school or classroom reform.

The College Board initiated its approach to early intervention in Fort Worth, Texas, in 1990; EQUITY 2000 currently affects approximately 500,000 students in more than 700 schools. Additional sites include Milwaukee, Wisconsin, Nashville, Tennessee, Prince Georges County, Maryland, Providence, Rhode Island, and San Jose, California.

American Indian Science and Engineering Society

As a national nonprofit organization, the American Indian Science and Engineering Society (AISES) seeks to encourage Native Americans to consider careers in science and technology. Its programs are funded by federal agencies such as the National Science Foundation and the Department of Education, and by numerous private and corporate foundations, including the DeWitt Wallace–*Reader's Digest* Foundation. It sponsors precollege summer academic programs at seven college and university campuses around the country. In 1996, over 350 middle and high school American Indian students from 55 tribes participated in the summer program (Barbic 1997). Participation in the summer program dramatically increases a student's probability of graduating from high school—from 52 percent for American Indians nationally to 90 percent for program participants (Barbic 1997). For those students who attended the summer programs for two years or more, over 50 percent are enrolled at institutions of higher education, compared to 17 percent of American Indians nationally. For the last 10 years, AISES also has held the National American Indian Science and Engineering Fair for elementary, middle high, and high school students. Attracting over 1,000 students annually, the fair requires students to develop a science research project that includes a research plan and application reviewed by a scientific review committee. The fair also offers students an opportunity to participate in group math competitions.

Project WINGS

One distinctive small-scale early intervention program is Project WINGS (Wise Investment in the Next Generation of Students) in Phoenix, Arizona. Founded in 1986 by a local chapter of Delta Kappa Gamma Society International, an organization of current and former educators, Project WINGS aims to increase students' and parents' involvement in the educative process. By offering financial assistance for post-secondary education, WINGS encourages parents to actively participate in the 12 years of their children's education before matriculation. The resulting program thus intervenes both academically and financially.

The inaugural program began with selected families from a kindergarten class in a school located in a lower socioeconomic area where few children went on to postsecondary education. The program requires parents to provide an atmosphere at home where students can study without distractions, to impart the benefits of education to their children, to promote good attendance, and to encourage the completion of homework. Additionally, parents are asked to attend Arizona Delta Kappa Gamma workshops on tutoring, counseling, and the education process in general. For their part, students must complete high school with grades and credits worthy of acceptance and registration in a state university. A student must enroll full time in an accredited institution of higher learning within two years of graduating from high school.*

When students successfully complete the program, Project WINGS divides the monies that are raised among the participating families and pays money directly to the students' institutions of choice. When the first crop of 26 WINGS students graduates from high school in 2000, WINGS Inc. hopes to provide a $10,000 scholarship for each successful family.

Regardless of the amount Project WINGS raises by 2000, the program is an impressive and perhaps unique example of an early intervention strategy that offers both academic and financial assistance and requires significant involvement from parents. Officers of Project WINGS report many inquiries about the program from other chapters of the organization in Arizona as well as in other states and even other countries.

---

* "Questions and Answers: Project WINGS." 1994. Phoenix, Arizona.

SCHOOL-COLLEGE COLLABORATION

The Traditional Separation between K–12 and Higher Education

The first figure presented in the 1995 edition of the annual *Digest of Education Statistics* is a schematic diagram of the American educational system (National Center 1995b). This diagram, which has been the initial figure in the annual *Digest* for many years, depicts two vertically arranged institutional clusters. The bottom one represents the elementary and secondary academic and vocational-technical systems, the top one the postsecondary systems, including college, university, professional, vocational, and technical education. The institutional types are connected within both clusters, but the clusters are shown as clearly separate; in fact, a solid horizontal line between the two clusters emphasizes the separation.

The schematic is symbolic of the historic dichotomy between the "compulsory" elementary and secondary level and the "elective" postsecondary level. The two levels differ significantly in purpose, funding, organization, and many other important aspects. Moreover, a sort of psychological and perceptual barrier separates the two systems. Since the mid-19th century, basic schooling has generally been perceived as necessary to the nation's civic and economic functioning. As a result, primary and secondary education has become universal, and attendance, by law, is mandatory. In contrast, postsecondary education has been historically exclusive, selective, and elitist. Even when the state universities with nominal tuition proliferated in the late 19th century, and when public junior colleges at the turn of the century began as tuition-free upward extensions of local high schools, enrollees were mainly the better students who could not afford to attend the more expensive and prestigious private colleges. Even these no-tuition, low-cost public colleges were somewhat elitist in that their attendees were mainly young people whose families could continue to support them and did not need the income a young person normally would contribute to the family when he or she began full-time employment immediately after compulsory schooling.

The K–16 Movement

The educational reform movement that began in the early 1980s has "school-college collaboration" as one of its major themes. As this theme has evolved, various forms of it have ranged from quite traditional, narrowly focused formal arrangements, usually of short duration, between K–12 schools and higher education, to drastic and permanent systemic change that essentially obliterates the traditional separation between the two levels. Collaboration of the latter type is related to early intervention in two ways. First, like early intervention, such collaboration often seeks to create a seamless transition from the beginning of schooling into the baccalaureate program. Some more extreme versions, for example, the "seamless web" model, envision the transition extending into doctoral and professional programs. Second, much of the collaboration between systems is aimed at alleviating the same problems that concern early intervention programs, namely, that failure to complete high school hampers low-income/minority students from participating in postsecondary education—with all that such exclusion implies for the future of these youth.

This subsection briefly reviews the background, progress, and current status of the main variations of collaboration between school and college, focusing on those that overlap with early intervention and academic outreach programs. Treatment of the collaboration is brief, because unlike other forms of early intervention, much has been, and is being, written on this burgeoning movement (see, e.g., Greenberg 1991) and because systemic school-college collaboration is a much broader movement that includes such topics as the revision of preparation of teachers and administrators, and new ways of allocating finances and other resources between systems at the state level. A review of the extant literature on school-college collaboration for the Education Commission of the States categorizes the movement as tending "to focus on . . . programs and services for students, programs and services for educators, research and resources, or restructuring of the educational system" (Wallace 1993, p. 2). This report deals only with programs and services for students, particularly with the need to increase aspirations for, and ease transitions into, higher education for all students as a concern for both K–12 and higher education, with the emphasis on easing transitions for the same types of students targeted by most early intervention programs. "These partnerships recognize demographics of the student population and the need to target efforts toward minority and at-risk students traditionally underserved by either institution" (p. 2). Many collaborative initiatives "include early intervention programs at the elementary, middle, or high school level, articulation agreements between the sectors, and accelerated programs offering college-level instruction" (p. 2).

Among accelerated programs are those referred to as "concurrent-enrollment models" (Greenberg 1991), such as the venerable Advanced Placement (AP) program begun by the College Board in 1955. From the beginning, AP offered college-level courses to well-prepared high school students. AP never focused on "historically underrepresented" students, although low-income/minority students can be included among "well-prepared" students served by the program. More than 200,000 students from about one-third of the nation's schools annually participate in the program. In addition to AP, examples of concurrent-enrollment programs include Syracuse University's Project Advance, which involves collaboration with local school districts, two state-level models (Minnesota and Florida), and two examples of community college–high school collaboration in the New York City area (Greenberg 1991). (See "Academic Outreach Programs," later in this report, for a discussion of "middle college" or "2+2" programs.)

A Nation at Risk

School-college collaboration, in its many forms and under its many names, received its original impetus from the national educational reform movement that began with publication of *A Nation at Risk* (U.S. National Commission 1983). That report, and those that followed in rapid succession within a few years, called for radical restructuring of traditional educational systems. The American Association for Higher Education (AAHE) was one of the first organizations to respond, and it has remained in the forefront. AAHE's annual national conference in October 1995 had as its theme "Accelerating Reform in Tough Times: Focus on Student Learning K–16." The preface to the conference program notes that:

> *AAHE has a long history in the area of school/college collaboration. At its 1981 National Conference on Higher Education, Ernest Boyer and others spoke of the need for schools and colleges to work together toward education and reform. In 1984, inspired by* A Nation at Risk *and a new wave in [educational] reform, AAHE*

. . . much of the collaboration between systems is aimed at alleviating the same problems that concern early intervention programs, namely, that failure to complete high school hampers low-income/ minority students from participating in postsecondary education—with all that such exclusion implies for the future of these youth.

dedicated that year's National Conference to school/college collaboration (American Association 1995, p. 10).

Education Trust
In 1990, AAHE established its Office of School/College Collaboration, and three years later, with the help of a large foundation grant, transformed that office into the current Education Trust. The trust continues to spearhead expanding systemic reforms in a number of ways (Haycock 1996). Staff of the trust are available to act as consultants in establishing local K–16 councils and in other activities. Among the trust's several goals is "increasing the number of postsecondary institutions and school districts working together with the broader community to improve the achievement of urban youth—especially minorities and the poor—through systemic reform strategies" (American Association 1995, p. 2).

Among the trust's many initiatives is the Community Compacts for Student Success project. Each compact is a multiyear agreement among a community's K–12 and higher education systems and other entities to "increase dramatically the number of poor and minority students who complete high school, enroll in postsecondary education, and persist to completion" (p. 2). Six cities currently have compacts: Birmingham, Alabama, El Paso, Texas, Hartford, Connecticut, Philadelphia, Pennsylvania, Providence, Rhode Island, and Pueblo, Colorado (Brown 1994).

Education Commission of the States
Three other national organizations have been actively promoting school-college collaboration but from somewhat different perspectives. The Education Commission of the States was founded in 1965 to assist state governments in improving education at all levels. In the 1980s, the commission analyzed and supported state policies and practices in building school-college partnerships, and in 1991 it established a project called "State Leadership for Partnerships: Building Bridges between Schools and Colleges."

The project commissioned two papers, among many other activities. The first (Gomez and de los Santos 1992) analyzes various state policies that foster and sustain collaboration; the second is the annotated bibliography on school-college partnerships cited earlier (Wallace 1993). Among the works noted in the bibliography is *What Works: School/*

College Partnerships to Improve Poor and Minority Student Achievement (Stoel, Togneri, and Brown 1992), an overview that divides partnerships into seven categories, including early identification and dropout programs and partnerships involving schools on college campuses.

State Higher Education Executive Officers

Another organization active in promoting school-college collaboration is State Higher Education Executive Officers (SHEEO), which focuses its attention on analyzing and encouraging leadership in collaboration by state-level higher education governing boards and coordinating commissions. In 1990, SHEEO published a report surveying the efforts in eight states, several of which focus their leadership in projects that include early intervention (Mingle and Rodriguez 1990). For example, Arizona's Minority Education Access and Achievement Cooperative provides planning grants for "collaborative programs that will extend the educational pipeline for minority students" (p. 7). One project in Colorado focuses on a system that accurately tracks students from any entry or exit point of educational activity. The rationale behind the project is that, before effective programs to promote minority achievement could be developed, the state "had to gain an understanding of the actual participation and achievement of minority students" (p. 12). Illinois and Massachusetts focus attention on the "transfer points" at which many students are lost, including the transition from grade school to middle school, from middle school to high school, and from high school to college. Montana developed a tracking system similar to Colorado's, but it is focused specifically on students in its American Indian population of over 50,000.

Council of Chief State School Officers

The Council of Chief State School Officers has, since the early 1990s, emphasized a number of early intervention initiatives, which include systemic changes in fostering school-to-college collaboration and "encouraging school success of children at risk [by guaranteeing] effective educational services" (Council 1997, p. 1). These and similar early intervention initiatives are coordinated through the council's Resource Center on Educational Equity, which "is responsible for managing and staffing a variety of council leadership initiatives to provide better educational services to children, especially those placed at risk of school failure" (p. 1). The center has emphasized liaisons with other organizations interested in early intervention, such as the American Association for the Advancement of Science and the Child Care Action Campaign.

FEDERAL AND STATE-SUPPORTED EARLY INTERVENTION

Early Federal Support

The federal government's involvement in early intervention programs began long before the 1992 federally mandated National Early Intervention Scholarship and Partnership Program. In 1965, President Lyndon B. Johnson's War on Poverty resulted in expanded access and support for populations previously underrepresented on college campuses. Central to the fight for access and equality were three special programs for students from disadvantaged backgrounds. These programs, widely referred to as the TRIO programs, include Upward Bound, Student Support Services, and Talent Search (see Wolanin 1997 for the history of the TRIO programs over three decades). In the first decade, during the 1960s, the first three TRIO programs were created. During the 1970s, the TRIO programs expanded to include Educational Opportunity Centers. "The critical decade for TRIO came in the eighties, which can be characterized as the decade of building permanence of the TRIO programs" (p. 2). Since the initial TRIO legislation, two more programs have been added to the federal government's early intervention efforts. The Training Program for Special Services Staff and Leadership Personnel and the Ronald E. McNair Postbaccalaureate Achievement Program, created in 1986, complete the roster of TRIO programs.

TRIO programs are available to Americans with household incomes of $24,000 or less. In 1994–95, at least one of the programs existed on over 1,200 campuses and in the aggregate served nearly 700,000 students on an FY 1995 budget of $463 million.* The Department of Education (DOE) is responsible for informing the public of eligibility requirements for TRIO and financial awards. The information appears in three media: written publications, computer software, and a telephone information hot line. DOE paper publications include *The Expected Family Contribution Formula Book: The Counselor's Handbook for High Schools* and *Preparing Your Child for College: A Resource Book for Parents*. Computer software entitled *The Student Aid Tour, The Estimator,* and *The Electronic Need Analysis System* helps students determine eligibility and calculate family contribution. Finally, DOE's toll-free telephone hot line fields over 2 million calls annually.

---

* "Introducing TRIO"—NCEOA brochure. 1995. Washington, D.C.

Upward Bound, the most widely recognized TRIO program, offers potential first-generation college students supplemental instruction in college preparatory classes. The nearly 600 programs currently operating in colleges and universities across the country offer on-campus instruction in literature, composition, mathematics, science, and foreign languages during the summer and on weekends. According to figures provided by the National Council of Educational Opportunity Associations (NCEOA), in 1994–95 over $171 million was spent on Upward Bound programs that assisted 44,700 students. During that same year, Upward Bound provided 81 math and science programs costing over $18 million that served 3,712 students.

Student Support Services (SSS), limited to first-generation college students, provides remedial education and counseling. The program aims to help students stay in college until completion of a degree. Currently, SSS is active on over 700 campuses nationwide. SSS programs served 165,561 students in 1994–95 at a cost of $143.5 million.

Talent Search provides counseling and guidance to students in grades 6 through 12. Participants receive information about financial aid, scholarships, and admissions practices. In 1994–95, 319 Talent Search programs based on college and university campuses served approximately 299,850 students with total expenditures of $78.8 million.

Although not strictly an early intervention program under NEISP's definition cited earlier, Educational Opportunity Centers (EOCs) are nonetheless members of the TRIO family. Seventy EOCs provide information about college choice and financial aid to prospective college students. The beneficiaries of this assistance, however, are for the most part displaced or underemployed workers rather than elementary and secondary students.* Such centers used $24.7 million in federal funds and aided 156,686 individuals in 1994–95.

The Ronald E. McNair Postbaccalaureate Achievement Program serves as an impetus for minority and low-income students to pursue careers in college teaching, achieving its goal by providing research opportunities and faculty mentorship for participants. In 1994–95, 98 programs served 2,461 students at a total cost of $21 million. Funds appropriated under this program can be used for academic support services for middle and high school students.

---

* "Introducing TRIO."

When working in concert, the TRIO programs form a complementary progression for needy students. The purpose of the TRIO programs is to help low-income students "to overcome class, social, academic, and cultural barriers to higher education" (National Council 1997, p. 1). Initially, promising students are identified (Talent Search), then prepared for the rigors of college-level academic work (Upward Bound), offered information on academic and financial aid opportunities (Educational Opportunity Centers), and, finally, as college students, offered tutoring and support (Student Support Services).*

The decisions made during the 1997 reauthorization of the Higher Education Act could potentially affect the fate of the TRIO programs into FY 2004 (Wolanin 1997, p. 3). "Part of the political history of the success of the TRIO [programs] over the last 20+ years has been that it has been the leadership of the committees that has fostered and believed in and advocated on behalf of the TRIO programs" (p. 4). Uncertainty exists about potential changes to TRIO that Congress could make because most experienced members of Congress have retired. Policy analysts like Wolanin believe, however, that the inexperienced 105th Congress should reauthorize the programs without making any substantial changes (p. 4). "The TRIO programs have evolved to the point where they are strong, stable, and . . . work well. They could always use more money, but in terms of basic legislative structure, they're in pretty good shape" (p. 4).

In another federal program not related to TRIO, the Higher Education Amendments of 1986 created the School, College, and University Partnership Program (SCUPP). It provides grants to two- and four-year colleges and to educational agencies to develop projects aiming to increase the academic skills of low-income secondary students. From the beginning, the federal government's financial commitment to SCUPP was designed to progressively decrease as infrastructures matured to self-sufficiency (Hexter 1990).

Federal and State Cost-Sharing Programs
Chapter 2 of the 1992 reauthorization of the Higher Education Act of 1965 establishes the National Early Intervention Scholarship and Partnership (NEISP) program. Central to the development of a mandated partnership program between

The decisions made during the 1997 reauthorization of the Higher Education Act could potentially affect the fate of the TRIO programs into FY 2004.

---

* "Introducing TRIO."

the federal government and the states is the conviction that higher education is best supported by the combined efforts of all parties involved in the educational process. In 1991, the University of Vermont's president, George Davis, stated in his testimony before a Senate hearing on early intervention, "Three constituencies will be critical to our success or failure—state and local government, the higher education community, and the federal government" (U.S. Senate 1991, p. 342).

Findings from a survey of 12 state early intervention programs (including a description of Georgia's HOPE program, which supports only students already enrolled in postsecondary education) summarize seven goals for early intervention programs:

> *(1) increase high school graduation rates and reduce school dropout rates, (2) increase enrollment of at-risk students in math and science courses, (3) ensure that high school graduates are prepared for work and for college, (4) increase college enrollment rates, particularly among disadvantaged youth, (5) encourage high school graduates to attend in-state colleges and universities, (6) increase college competition rates among the state's students, and (7) improve the overall quality of life for state residents* (Perna 1995, pp. 33–34).

State Implementation of NEISP

NEISP serves as an impetus for states to further their early intervention programs. Earlier, the federal government used rewards in its efforts to set up state-based student aid programs. In 1973, Congress provided the State Student Incentive Grant (SSIG) program, which offered matching funds as rewards to states that established their own student aid programs. Before SSIG, only 24 states had established programs, but within four years of the incentive's introduction, all states had established programs.

From a modest initial appropriation of $200 million in FY 1993, the appropriation for NEISP nearly doubled in the second year. In the stringent budget cutbacks for FY 1995, however, appropriation of new funds fell to $3.1 million, with the predictable effect on state programs. In FY 1995, DOE provided continuation awards to the six original 1994–95 grant awardees; therefore, only about $1 million was available to award to new 1995–96 grant applicants (U.S. Dept. of Education 1995, p. 1).

Analysis of applications and the ultimate award of grant dollars is a highly competitive process and the duty of the Secretary of Education. Each state that wishes to participate must submit an application to the Department of Education, a narrative that addresses program implementation, and the usual required federal disclosure forms.

In FY 1995, successful applicants included six states with continuing programs—California, Indiana, Maryland, New Mexico, Vermont, and Washington—and three new award-ees—Minnesota, Rhode Island, and Wisconsin. For FY 1996, NEISP's budget was increased by only $500,000, to $3.6 million. Consequently, no new awards were made and the funds are being used to continue programs in the same nine states.

These programs vary in many details related to particular demographic, economic, institutional, and political variables, but all include a number of basic NEISP principles. They offer some degree of counseling with regard to educational and employment options and opportunities. Students are encouraged to investigate career options that they might not have considered. The programs generally afford some type of mentoring and tutoring by upper-level students in middle and high schools and by college students. Academic support, workshops, and other activities are provided to introduce students and their families to educational and job opportunities. Some of the programs also offer, and may guarantee, scholarships for higher education to students who graduate from high school. Such scholarships are generally provided for public institutions of higher education, but in some instances they also allow support in private institutions.

The programs are mostly designed for at-risk students and may start as early as grade school and continue through the senior year of high school. The goals include a reduction in school dropouts through provision of a safety net of services and encouragement. Preparation for the job market is emphasized, and, in particular, students from low-income families are assisted in seeking enrollment in college. Some programs emphasize assistance to students of the first generation in their families to attend college. Many programs include special activities to discourage the use of drugs and alcohol.

Special attention is also given to students with limited proficiency in English and to students with physical disabilities. Some programs have introduced a student pledge to work toward graduation from high school, to achieve a grade point average of 2.0 or better, to meet college admission requirements, and to apply for admission and financial aid. Family involvement is stressed, and a community-based approach builds a sense of involvement and proprietorship of the program as a basis for sustaining and continuing participation.

The following paragraphs briefly describe the nine existing NEISP programs.

California

The Early Intervention Scholarship and Partnership Program in California is one of the six initial programs awarded federal matching funds. This program begins with students in the fourth grade and follows them through the senior year of high school. Addressing the needs of disadvantaged students at the community level, the program served 7,862 students in 1994–95 through counseling, mentoring, and academic support. It does not include a scholarship component.

Indiana

Indiana was one of the first states to take part in the federal program through establishment of the Twenty-First Century Scholars Program. The program's goals are to reduce the number of school dropouts, increase preparedness for the job market, encourage low-income students to enter college, decrease drug and alcohol use, increase individual economic productivity, and enhance the quality of life. The program offers support to selected eighth graders to help defray the costs of attending public or private postsecondary institutions. Students are guaranteed support for four years beyond high school graduation, and they may use the scholarships for public or private tuition. Participants are required to pledge that they will abide by stated academic and social codes of conduct. The program served 2,000 students in 1995.

Maryland

Administered under the auspices of the Maryland Higher Education Commission, Maryland's College Preparation

Intervention Program pays particular attention to Maryland middle school students who otherwise would not consider attending college; the program thus provides a safety net of academic and counseling services for students at risk of dropping out of school.

Minnesota

Minnesota's program, to be administered by the Minnesota Education Services Office, is yet to be implemented. Services will be provided through local community-based and ethnic-specific organizations. Fourth and fifth graders who have at least one of five risk factors (at risk of dropping out, a member of a low-income family, first generation to attend college, limited proficiency in English, a disability) will be offered career counseling and other opportunities to enhance awareness of educational employment options.

New Mexico

The program, whose slogan is "I can dream it, I can do it," provides guaranteed financial assistance to attend public institutions of higher learning and offers workshops and activities aimed at expanding the horizons of at-risk elementary students. It emphasizes keeping students in school, improving academic performance and graduation rates, and encouraging college attendance and new career aspirations. The program currently serves 325 students.

Rhode Island

The Children's Crusade for Higher Education set an early example as one of the first in the nation to offer educational intervention services and scholarships. Administered by a private nonprofit organization with no state oversight, the program offers services in collaboration with local community organizations. Students are chosen from neighborhoods with high concentrations of low-income families, and participants are required to make a pledge stating they will abide by stated academic and social codes of conduct. More than 14,500 students currently participate.

Vermont

Administered under the auspices of the Vermont Student Assistance Corporation, Future Start provides a broad base of support services emphasizing exploration of postsecondary educational programs and career opportunities. All students in the program are of the first generation in their family to attend college. Participants must maintain a 2.8 grade point average or show a 10 percent improvement for the period of their involvement in the program. Financial need is a factor in awarding scholarships. During 1994, its first year, the program served 500 students.

Washington

Administered by the Washington State Higher Education Coordinating Board, Washington's program emphasizes a community-based approach for the delivery of support services and scholarships. Services are provided in communities where students live, and students are expected to improve themselves as well as their neighborhoods. Additionally, the program emphasizes intense community and family/parental involvement. Participants are required to make a pledge stating they will abide by stated academic and social codes of conduct. The 150 students who participated in 1996 reflected the diversity of their communities.

Wisconsin

The state formed an umbrella organization to oversee a variety of outreach programs, including NEISP. The program's general goal is to identify and provide guidance and support for at-risk students. Specifically, it provides counseling aimed at raising students' confidence and offers follow-up programs in collaboration with higher education institutions. Bilingual education is also offered as part of the program.

Other State Programs

Many other states support one or more early intervention programs. A number of them also submitted proposals for inclusion in NEISP but were denied funding. This subsection reviews six state programs. Overall, information was gathered from over 20 states in addition to the nine NEISP states.

The information gathered suggests that a complete census of state early intervention programs, although highly desirable, would be difficult to achieve for at least two reasons. First, such programs are dispersed for administrative control across many different types of entities, for example, state financial aid agencies, departments of education, coordinating agencies, systems of higher education institutions, and even (in the case of Rhode Island) a privately controlled foundation. Second, the programs themselves are often quite transitory; they change purpose, scope, and administrative control according to the vagaries of state funding levels and the availability or withdrawal of federal matching funds, partisan political support, and other factors.

Two of the following six programs are described in somewhat more detail than the others because they seem to typify many of the goals and changing fortunes of state early intervention programs: Arizona's ASPIRE program and Hawaii's Project HOPE (with its two related programs).

Arizona's ASPIRE program

The Arizona Student Program Investing Resources for Education (ASPIRE) sets aside tuition scholarship funds for Arizona public school students who intend to pursue postsecondary education. The laws that established ASPIRE provide student and institutional criteria, standards, and procedures for administration of the program. A selection committee comprising nine members—three appointed by the governor, three by the Arizona Commission for Postsecondary Education (ACPE), and three by the State Board of Education—fine-tunes the standards for participation. The committee determines the eligibility of schools with the approval of ACPE and develops criteria for financial need to determine students' eligibility for participation.

The legislation allows the state treasury to establish a fund administered by ACPE as a source of scholarships for students who participate in the program. The sources of the fund are expected to be both legislative appropriations and private or public donations. Scholarships for tuition are available to students who wish to attend any postsecondary institution in the state, with the amount determined on the basis of average tuition costs at Arizona public universities.

ASPIRE was fashioned after Eugene Lang's I Have A Dream program and Louisiana's Taylor Plan (see the description following), both of which began as private investments in education by wealthy philanthropists and later became the inspirations for larger, publicly supported endeavors. ASPIRE's primary goal is to encourage low-income elementary school students who show academic progress to remain in school and continue to postsecondary education. Elementary schools throughout Arizona compete to be designated as Project ASPIRE schools. Third grade students from the designated schools who meet the established financial and academic criteria are eligible to participate.

The Arizona House of Representatives has appropriated $300,000 for ASPIRE, although the legislature expects and requires ACPE to solicit and obtain matching funds. Financial resources for ASPIRE have not yet reached the level required for implementation, and it is likely that a pilot program will be implemented to determine whether a full-scale program can be effective and the potential level of support from private and public benefactors.

Hawaii's HOPE and related programs

Hawaii's several early intervention programs are interrelated but have different emphases. They have experienced changing levels of support related to changes in the overall economy. The University of Hawaii (UH), a unified system that includes all postsecondary public institutions and campuses, initiated Operation Manong in 1972 to provide support services for disadvantaged students to ensure equal access to higher education. It was the first such program.

In 1987, the Pre-Freshman Enrichment Project (PREP) started under Operation Manong, with 20 seventh graders invited to a summer program at the Manoa campus. The Manoa campus is the research-oriented unit of UH, and PREP was begun with a federal grant to encourage Filipino and Native Hawaiian children to consider engineering-related fields. In 1989, UH assumed support of the program.

UH also operates a statewide outreach program called *Na Pua No'eau* with federal funds. The program is now in its fourth year and currently receives $1.2 million in federal money. It focuses mainly on Native Hawaiian children and is administered under the university's Center for Gifted and Talented Native Hawaiian Children. Its overall goal is to raise the educational and career aspirations of Native Hawaiian children. The program offers nine components to schoolchildren from kindergarten through high school, ranging from single-day events (Super Enrichment Saturdays) to a year-round program of curricular enrichment and mentoring. Federal funding is uncertain beyond 1997, and the current state funding level of $140,000 will be reviewed at that time.

HOPE (the Hawaiian Opportunity Program in Education) is the state's largest commitment to early intervention to date. It has undergone significant changes in structure and support since its inception in 1990. At that time, the legislature committed $1 million each year for 10 years to be set aside to form an endowment, the interest from which was to be available for scholarships to attract underrepresented minority students to UH. Specific groups targeted are African Americans (2.6 percent of the school population, 1 percent of UH enrollment), Filipino (19 percent and 8 percent, respectively), and Native Hawaiian (23 percent and 6 percent, respectively). The operational plan in 1991 was for HOPE to begin with all third graders in 15 low-income/minority schools and then to provide scholarships for them when they enrolled in UH in 2001. In 1995, however, the state's financial problems caused the legislature to terminate all appropriations to the HOPE endowment and to move all funds it had deposited in the endowment to the general fund to cover revenue shortages. According to UH officials, the state resumed financial support for the program in 1997, but at a lower level than the original commitment.

Louisiana's Taylor program

After speaking to a group of 147 at-risk students attending Livingston Middle School in New Orleans, Patrick Taylor, a self-made millionaire, was convinced that the students needed to believe they could afford college so they would work hard to stay in school. Taylor promised a full scholarship for tuition plus all expenses to all students who meet the academic standards and social codes of conduct required by the program.

Taylor convinced the state of Louisiana to adopt a statewide program known as the Taylor Plan. Under the plan, any Louisiana resident under the age of 18 from a family earning below $25,000 annually is eligible for a full-tuition scholarship at a state university if he or she takes 17.5 credit hours in a college preparatory curriculum, maintains at least a 2.5 grade point average in those courses, and scores at least 18 on the American College Test.

New York's Liberty Scholarship
And Partnership Program

Inspired by the I Have A Dream program, New York Governor Mario Cuomo in 1988 proposed a comprehensive plan to make a college education possible for all of New York's disadvantaged students. Thus were developed the Liberty Scholarships, whose purpose was to provide grants to help pay for a student's nontuition college expenses at any state university or city university branch if the student's family earned below $26,000 annually. To be eligible, students had to apply for a federal Pell grant and a New York Tuition Assistance Program grant to pay for tuition. In addition, the student was required to be under 22 years of age, enter college within two years of receiving a high school diploma or GED, and meet the requirements for citizenship and residency.

The New York State Liberty Scholarship and Partnership Program provided students at risk of dropping out of school with services specifically designed to keep them in school through high school graduation, to encourage them to enroll in higher education, and/or to secure meaningful employment. The program also awarded grants to help colleges and community-based organizations set up counseling, mentoring, and support services for Liberty Scholarship students. New York's fiscal problems, however, caused both the scholarship and partnership programs to be cut from the budget in 1991.

North Carolina's Legislative College Opportunity Program

This program, now in its third year of operation, was established by the state legislature to, as stated in the 1994 law, "recruit new students to enroll in college in future years who might not be able to attend college without incentives." It was preceded by the 1993 Freshman Scholars Program, which offered high school seniors financial support to attend one of the five historically black campuses of the University of North Carolina.

The Freshman Scholars Program was subsumed under the College Opportunity Program, which offered financial, educational, and social support services to middle and high school students to encourage improved academic performance and persistence. The first full year's appropriation of $800,000 was divided equally among the university's 16 campuses. Each campus is required to establish an administrative unit that works with school districts in the geographic region it serves.

Oklahoma's Higher Learning Access Program

The original intent of the 1992 legislation that created this program was to establish a trust fund, the proceeds of which were to provide up to five years of financial assistance for eligible students to attend one of the state's public higher education institutions. Sufficient funds to establish an endowment were not appropriated, however. An appropriation of $200,000 was made in FY 1995 to serve a number of students who were ninth graders in 1992. These students and their families had been informed of the program, and the appropriation enabled the students to carry through on their plans to enroll in college when they graduated from high school.

The program is need-based and also requires students to achieve a 2.5 grade point average in high school and to meet behavioral standards, such as refraining from drug use and criminal activity. The state legislature appropriated $1.4 million to provide financial assistance for 636 eligible high school seniors who graduated in June 1996 and a similar amount for eligible June 1997 graduates. State officials indicate that the state plans to continue funding at a level adequate to support the program for at least the next several years.

ACADEMIC OUTREACH PROGRAMS

Many colleges and universities, particularly those that serve urban populations with large and growing proportions of minorities, are increasingly concerned about effectively serving at-risk youth. These institutions' concerns center around academically serving the society that sustains them as well as maintaining adequate enrollment in their own interest.

This section focuses on institutional academic outreach programs from three perspectives. First, it discusses a 1994 national survey of 850 institutions (Chaney, Lewis, and Farris 1995) sponsored by the National Center for Education Statistics and an in-depth survey (Stout 1990) of the outreach programs of 10 institutions, and includes a brief appendix listing the academic outreach initiatives of 27 other colleges and universities. Second, it briefly describes outreach programs offered by a large public research university (Arizona State University) and by a prominent private university (University of Southern California). Third, it discusses the concept of a systemic interface between high schools and public community colleges.

Two Surveys of Institutional Academic Outreach Programs

In 1994, the U.S. Department of Education commissioned the Survey on Precollegiate Programs for Disadvantaged Students at Higher Education Institutions. The survey was conducted through the postsecondary education quick-information system, a specialized sampling of the comprehensive Integrated Postsecondary Education Data System operated by the National Center for Education Statistics. This survey exemplifies the definition of academic outreach used in this report in that it "concentrated on precollegiate programs that are operated by higher education institutions, although the sponsor of the program might be outside the institution (such as the federal government or a private institution)" (Chaney, Lewis, and Farris 1995, p. 3).

A total of 813 institutions provided information about their largest (in terms of funding) precollegiate program for disadvantaged students (Chaney, Lewis, and Farris 1995, p. 57). The study found that about one-third (32 percent) of the surveyed institutions offered at least one program for precollegiate students in 1993–94 and that, among those institutions, 31 percent listed Upward Bound as the largest program (p. 7).

The institutions noted that the top three program goals were "increasing the likelihood of the students' attending college (78 percent), increasing general academic skills development (67 percent), and increasing retention in or completion of high school (64 percent)" (p. iii). The majority of the students participating in the programs were high school students (64 percent), with junior high school students accounting for the next largest group (25 percent) (p. 39). Students in the institutions' largest programs were most likely to be from low-income families (68 percent), female (59 percent), and African American (39 percent) or Hispanic (29 percent) (pp. 31–32).

The 260 institutions with precollegiate programs served 317,400 students in 1993–94 (p. 11) and involved approximately 9,600 faculty and 13,500 students who worked with the program (p. 14). The sample of 850 surveyed institutions was constructed to represent the total of 3,470 institutions in the quick-information system roster of two- and four-year colleges and universities.

The survey was purely descriptive rather than analytical or comparative. Nonetheless, it provides useful normative information about the scope (numbers of students served, program staff, and so on) of the largest precollegiate programs of academic outreach operated across the country.

In the other survey analyzed for this report, Stout (1990) reviewed the findings of a survey of 10 urban four-year colleges and universities actively engaged in outreach programs for minority youth. The institutions, judged to be relatively successful in recruiting and graduating such youth, are Brooklyn College, California State University at Dominguez Hills, Florida International University, Florida State University, Memphis State University, Temple University, University of California at Los Angeles, University of New Mexico, University of Texas at El Paso, and Wayne State University. In reviewing these 10 institutions' efforts at early intervention, Stout compared them to a three-part strategic framework (Whiteley and Lacy 1985). The first strategy is a "talent search" that identifies and recruits the most able minority students. The second strategy is "mediation," in which the college or university offers specialized programs for underprepared minority youth to enable them to succeed in the higher education environment. The third strategy tends to focus on institutional self-interest and assumes that the relative decline in the pool of nonminority youth aged 18 to 22 will necessitate a search for new clientele. The rapidly growing pool of minority youth presents an obvious opportunity, especially for urban institutions surrounded by public school systems becoming predominantly attended by historically underrepresented racial and ethnic groups. It is to the institution's advantage if it can succeed in helping local schools increase retention and graduation. In addition, the higher education institution is well served if it can help the neighborhood schools increase the academic aptitude and achievement of their minority graduates.

All the foregoing strategies involve proactive academic outreach; the 10 institutions surveyed share six overall "postures" that assist in successfully recruiting and graduating minority youth:

1. Minority groups' achievement is viewed as a problem with preparation rather than a racial problem.
2. Campus environment is a critical factor in students' involvement and success.
3. Small numbers of minority faculty and limited involvement in equal opportunity programs by all faculty members are problems needing urgent attention.
4. The administration is visibly committed to academic outreach.
5. Strategies for promoting the success of minority students (in predominantly white institutions) or for promoting the success of all students (in multicultural institutions) are comprehensive and systematic rather than fragmented and sporadic.
6. The most progress has occurred in universities where institutional commitment and good educational practices are enhanced by favorable state policy (Stout 1990).

The academic outreach programs of the urban institutions surveyed can be classified as three types: (1) unilateral, or controlled predominantly by the institution, (2) institutional assistance or organization of community programs, and (3) collaboration with the public sector (Stout 1990). The first type usually involves talent searches similar to, for example, the institutes offered by Wayne State University and California State University at Dominguez Hills to students as young as 9 as well as their parents. Both universities also mounted "early outreach" programs to inform talented youth about opportunities to attend college (Memphis State and UCLA also offered such programs).

Several universities, including Temple, UCLA, and Florida International University, worked closely with community minority advocacy groups on the common goals of recruiting minority youth. UCLA, Temple, Memphis State, and California State University–Dominguez Hills fostered collaboration with the public sector, especially with school systems and local community colleges.

Several universities, including Temple, UCLA, and Florida International University, worked closely with community minority advocacy groups on the common goals of recruiting minority youth.

The scope of institutional outreach in this sample and across the nation is "relatively small" as a result of, among other factors, "the historic division of responsibility across K–12, community college, and university missions" (Stout 1990, p. 30). This "historic division" is beginning to erode, however, and the wide range of academic outreach activities reviewed in the appendix to this report may signal the rapid expansion of such programs. Another indication that academic outreach is expanding is now found on the Internet. The Academic Outreach homepage on the World Wide Web lists several examples of school-college collaboration.* The main thrust of the contents pertains to school-college collaboration in distance education and in joint teacher training projects, but several early intervention projects are found under the headings "community and two-year colleges" and "K–12."

One of the problems in assessing the actual scope of academic outreach is the lack of a reliable national survey of such activities. The closest found to such a resource are two directories, the first, published by the American Council on Education, a directory of college and university programs, projects, and services for historically underrepresented students (Mintz 1993), and the second a more recent directory published by the American Association for Higher Education (Wilbur and Lambert 1996). The range of activities among the more than 800 colleges and universities listed in ACE's directory is very broad; more than 50 institutions offer at least one or more programs that are clearly "academic outreach" as defined earlier. (The appendix contains descriptions of 33 programs in 27 institutions deemed representative of the extremely wide range of outreach programs—not

---

*URL: *www.outreach.umich.edu.* Contents copyright by the University of Michigan.

including participation in the federal TRIO programs, which are discussed earlier.) The programs included in the appendix are clearly unique. In the aggregate, they illustrate the creative and diverse efforts in this burgeoning field.* AAHE's directory focuses on school-to-college partnerships but also covers many other types of early intervention programs related to such partnerships.

Two Institutional Examples of Academic Outreach
This subsection describes the variety and range of academic outreach programs at two large urban universities. The purposes of these descriptions are to demonstrate that such programs can originate from almost any entity within the institution and pursue any kind of goals for early intervention, and that the diverse and diffuse nature of the programs makes institutional coordination exceedingly difficult. Some programs emanate from a single academic department, others from larger academic units like professional colleges. Still others are initiated by relatively small administrative units within student affairs; some involve much larger units or a combination of various-size units. Funding also varies widely. Both universities have federal TRIO institutional programs, but other programs may be funded by institutional, private, state, or civic organizations or by foundations or by any combination of these sources. Still others operate almost entirely on volunteer help donated by faculty, staff, and/or students.

Given this bewildering variety of origins, goals, and funding, it is not surprising that, to the best of our knowledge, no single source of information is available about all academic outreach programs in either institution. Any large university is essentially a conglomerate of several administrative domains, many of which are only loosely coordinated with one another or, at the very least, pursue separate goals with little incentive to collaborate. The separation between academic and student affairs programs has always existed to some degree in higher education institutions. And competition among academic units mitigates against coordination. For example, a foundation may request proposals for

---

*Readers interested in obtaining more information about any of the programs should consult the directory, which lists staff names and addresses for each program as it existed in 1993, when information was gathered for the directory.

funding to identify and recruit area minority youth who demonstrate high academic promise in mathematics and science. The academic unit that wins the grant would have little incentive to share potential students with such rare talent with other departments. The final section of this report discusses the benefits of, prospects for, and strategies for increasing coordination within an institution.

No claim is made for the representativeness or generalizability of these programs to other institutions. The two universities were selected mainly for convenience and access. All of the coauthors were located at one of the institutions during the drafting of the manuscript, and one of the coauthors had strong ties to the other institution. Both institutions are Research I universities located in very large metropolitan areas that are natural breeding grounds for academic outreach to at-risk youth.

Nevertheless, the two institutions differ significantly in some ways. Arizona State University is publicly controlled, the University of Southern California privately controlled. ASU is located in suburban Tempe in a middle-class residential area, USC in urban Los Angeles at the center of the Los Angeles metropolitan area. ASU's outreach is to a wide geographic region, while USC is closer to its at-risk neighbors.

Descriptions of the outreach programs for the two universities vary in level of detail. All information in the descriptions came from program publications and/or personal communications with program staff. The descriptions do not offer a comprehensive overview of outreach programs in either institution; they were selected to illustrate the range of academic outreach in these two universities.

Outreach programs at Arizona State University
- *Achieving a College Education (ACE).* ACE provides community college and high school students an opportunity to interact with faculty, staff, and advisers during five weeks on campus in the summer. The program offers workshops in educational success and social activities, and gives students an opportunity to live in residential halls. Participants must have completed English 101 or the equivalent.
- *Faculty Ambassadors.* The Arizona Board of Regents implemented the Faculty Ambassadors program to help disseminate information about changes in admissions requirements and information about the preparation of

college-bound students. The program offers the services of university faculty to area high schools and encourages a dialogue between high school and university educators. It is no longer funded by the Arizona Board of Regents but continues as a university initiative staffed by faculty volunteers.

- *Financial Aid and Academic Planning (FAAP).* FAAP is responsible for assisting students and their parents in the selection of high school courses and for providing information about available financial assistance. The program conducts school, home, and community workshops, serving 75 schools and reaching approximately 40,000 students annually.

- *Hispanic Mother-Daughter Program.* Recruiting 50 mother-daughter teams per semester, the Hispanic Mother-Daughter Program orients eighth graders (students must be in the eighth grade when they enter the program) and their mothers to higher education. It emphasizes the preparation and commitment required for scholastic achievement, the characteristics of campus life, the benefits of exploring various careers, and the development of self-esteem. Offering programs aimed at the enhancement of Hispanic parental commitment to higher education, the program provides a support network of school counselors, community leaders, and professional role models.

- *Parents as Partners.* This program promotes the notion that parents are their children's first and most important teachers. Through program-sponsored activities for parents at community agencies, parents learn to function as successful advocates of education, to create a home environment that reinforces and expands learning, to communicate with teachers, and to evaluate curricula. Parents as Partners is coordinated with privately financed and community-sponsored programs.

- *Seamless Web.* The Seamless Web project fosters achievement for ethnic minority graduates from disadvantaged social and academic backgrounds. It identifies 120 promising ethnic minority students in grades 11 and 12, provides financial, academic, and other types of support services through two years of community college, and selects 25 of the highest-achieving students to receive support through the completion of their master's and doctoral degrees.

- *Testskills.* Testskills, a 15-week course for high school sophomores, prepares students to take the standardized tests necessary for college admission and/or scholarships. It familiarizes students with the format of the PSAT, SAT, and ACT. Implemented in 25 schools, Testskills operates through a variety of community-based social service agencies.
- *Undergraduate admissions projects.* The Office of Undergraduate Programs at ASU sponsors several programs aimed at recruiting underrepresented students from area high schools. *Success Express* is a series of on-campus visits to Maricopa County high schools whose student populations are significantly underrepresented in higher education. The program includes motivational speakers, academic presentations, and campus tours. *EXCEL* is a recruitment program for the top 10 percent of Arizona high school students. It includes a three-credit-hour class, workshops, campus tours, and the experience of living on campus. The *Minority Parents Outreach Committee* is a committee of the ASU Parents Association that provides support for parents of ASU minority students and assists in outreach activities.
- *Upward Bound.* ASU's Upward Bound program, a federally funded TRIO program designed to increase the academic skills and motivational levels of low-income high school students and potential first-generation college students, provides "college simulation" through a six-week summer residential program that includes tutoring, advisement, counseling, and enrollment in college-credit courses. Eligible students are first-semester high school juniors at the time of admission. Participants must demonstrate financial need and the ability to benefit from postsecondary education. About 110 students participate in ASU Upward Bound each year.
- *Algebridge.* Algebridge is an accelerated math program for seventh and eighth graders developed by the College Board and the Educational Testing Service. The curriculum, developed and offered in collaboration with ASU math faculty, introduces students to algebraic thinking and prepares them to succeed in high school algebra courses. The program is used in 55 Arizona elementary schools and two community-based organizations and currently involves approximately 8,000 students.

- *Arizona Mathematics, Engineering, Science Achievement (MESA) program.* MESA is designed to develop a pool of minority high school students who are academically prepared to enter postsecondary math, engineering, or science programs. Participation begins in junior high school, with students selected through the use of a math interest survey. Services include peer tutoring and academic workshops on taking tests, critical thinking, and study skills. Students must maintain at least a 2.50 grade point average in required math, science, and English classes.
- *Summer Bridge Minority Engineering Program (MEP).* This program is aimed at reducing the dropout rate of beginning engineering students by enrolling prospective freshmen in a two-week residential bridge program. The focus is on prospective minority students in the College of Engineering and Applied Sciences (CEAS), who have traditionally experienced high dropout rates. The program works in conjunction with the academic departments of CEAS to offer students a comprehensive evaluation of their academic accomplishments and goals. It provides tutorial services to minority students based on their needs and offers mandatory academic advisement and peer counseling. MEP is operated in conjunction with the Coalition to Increase Minority Degrees; it also sponsors the Sun Devil Summer Bridge Program, which is a five-week program offering courses in technical communications and an introduction to engineering.
- *Math-Science Honors Program.* The Math-Science Honors Program is designed to address a shortage of minority students in academic fields requiring a strong base in mathematics and science. Minority high school students are selected for participation based on their grades in science and math courses, their teachers' recommendations, and personal interviews. They earn university credit in math and science classes. Courses are offered in two five-week sessions and one eight-week summer session. Tutoring and support services are also provided.
- *Women in Applied Science and Engineering (WISE).* In 1993, the College of Engineering and Applied Sciences at ASU began a deliberate effort to recruit, retain, and graduate female students. WISE, a summer program targeting female high school students and their teachers, gives precollege students a hands-on introduction to engineer-

ing and technology. Funded through grants from the College of Engineering and Applied Sciences and the National Science Foundation, WISE encourages high school students to consider engineering and science majors when they enter college.

- *Concurrent Enrollment Program.* This large-scale program enables high school students in the Phoenix metropolitan area to take courses in high school that also earn up to two years of credit at ASU. Offered through Rio Salado Community College (one of the colleges in the Maricopa County Community College District), the program involves all six Tempe Union high schools plus 12 other metropolitan area high schools. Students, who are typically honor students already enrolled in college preparatory programs, enter ASU as transfer students rather than first-time freshmen. The program enrolls over 2,000 students per year.

- *Promise of Progress (POP).* Founded in January 1997 by an ASU undergraduate student, POP is a mentoring program aimed at African-American male junior and senior high school students. Modeled after the highly successful 100 Black Men of America program, ASU's program matches ASU students with the younger students, much like a Big Brother program. ASU mentoring students bring the younger African-American male students on campus; the one-on-one mentoring capitalizes on the narrow generation gap between ASU undergraduates and junior and senior high school students.

Outreach programs at the University Of Southern California

- *Educational Talent Search Program.* ETSP helps participants develop the academic and motivational skills necessary to become better students, graduate from high school or obtain a GED, and enroll in college. ETSP is a TRIO program funded by a grant from the U.S. DOE. It serves 1,200 students from south central Los Angeles and Inglewood. Eligible students must attend one of 13 designated junior high schools and high schools or must live in one of three designated housing projects. Participation in the program, which provides a variety of academic and social services, is free.

- *Joint Educational Project (JEP).* JEP is a partnership of USC and seven local elementary schools, a middle school, a high school, an adult school, a nearby learning center, senior centers, and area health-care facilities. It offers teaching, tutoring, counseling, and health-care assistance to area residents, and provides practical and academic experiences for more than 1,400 USC students each year. USC students receive credit for participation in one of four programs: the teachers assistant program, the mentors program, health programs, and minicourses.

- *Neighborhood Academic Initiative.* The Neighborhood Academic Initiative delivers educational and social services to low-income, minority students and families residing in communities contiguous to USC. It administers five related programs: the USC Precollege Enrichment Academy, the Family Development Institute, the Outreach Program, the Retention Program, and the Research and Development Program. The initiative provides financial assistance and workshops on academic and personal issues, including academic advising, tutoring, and counseling. The program also includes a self-assessment component.

- *Norman Topping Student Aid Fund.* NTSAF is a student-supported, student-run scholarship program for low-income students living in the communities closest to USC. Students are required to perform at least 20 hours of community service per semester working in local schools as tutors, peer counselors, playground aides, and teacher's aides.

- *Peer Counseling Program.* USC's Peer Counseling Program is funded through the Office of Admissions. It focuses on recruiting students from targeted high schools in neighborhoods adjacent to the USC campus. USC students spend 10 to 20 hours per week helping minority and nontraditional students apply to college and secure financial aid. Peer counselors interact with high school counselors to provide information to students about access to the University of California, California State University, private colleges and universities in the state, and the California community colleges.

- Student Committee on Admissions and Recruitment. SCOAR gives presentations to local high school students to help educate them about what is needed to pursue a degree in higher education. SCOAR volunteers give the presentations; many of them also guide campus tours. Students can choose to tour residence halls, libraries, and other campus locations; they can have lunch with USC students, sit in on a class, or meet with an academic adviser.

- *Upward Bound project.* In operation since 1977, USC's nationally recognized Upward Bound program concentrates on serving 132 low-income, first-generation students between the ages of 13 and 19, including those who may be physically challenged. All services are provided free to eligible students, who must be enrolled in one of the designated high schools, meet the requirements for income, and/or be potential first-generation college students. The program offers advice about admissions and financial aid, preparation for testing, and academic advising. Students live on campus for six weeks.
- *Building Relationships to Insure Greater Educational Success.* BRIDGES is a Community Enterprise project administered through the Entrepreneur Program in USC's School of Business Administration. Each program iteration lasts two years, during which USC undergraduate business students volunteer to mentor seventh and eighth graders from a local middle school. School administrators and program coordinators identify and select BRIDGES students in the seventh grade. The program encompasses recreational, educational, and entrepreneurial experiences.

- *Young Entrepreneur Program.* YEP is a Community Enterprise project administered through the Entrepreneur Program in USC's School of Business Administration. The year-long program begins during the summer and continues through the school year. It provides entrepreneurial training and mentoring relationships for high school students in the community; with assistance from MBA candidates, YEP students start and manage their own small businesses.
- *Exploration of Architecture.* The Exploration of Architecture program is a one- or three-week summer residential program that offers a variety of activities related to the study and practice of architecture. USC faculty and students act as studio advisers to about 60 high school students from across the country, 10 of whom are disadvantaged youths sponsored through scholarships. Participants complete a design project and tour areas of architectural significance in Los Angeles.

- *Mathematics, Engineering, Science Achievement.* MESA aims to motivate and prepare at-risk high school and younger students to pursue math-based college education and careers. It provides field trips, speakers, weekly meetings, study support, summer programs, and competitions. Teachers who participate benefit from advice on the curriculum, program materials, and specialized training.
- *Marketplace in the Schools.* The Entrepreneur Program and KUSC (USC's radio station) are currently developing, in conjunction with the history–social science consultant for the Los Angeles County Office of Education, a curriculum program based on Marketplace, KUSC's nationally distributed business news program designed to enhance the study of economics in 12th grade. The curriculum consists of five modules corresponding to the five broad economic areas defined in the California History–Social Science Framework for Grade 12.
- *Pre-College Summer Art Program.* The Pre-College Summer Art Program is a Saturday-only art program designed to give high school artists the opportunity for hands-on study with professional artists. The program lasts for 15 weeks and allows participants to show their work in a public arena. All students enrolled in public high schools within a five-mile radius of USC are eligible to participate.
- *Educational Excellence for Children with Environmental Limitations.* This program is a partnership involving developers, local schools, and USC's School of Education that seeks to build a closer link among home, school, and community services. It provides precollege educational preparation, social service referrals, and college financial assistance for children from low-income housing located near the campus. The complex, opened in 1992 in south Los Angeles, houses 42 tenants and will serve 80-plus children. Doctoral interns serve as on-site tutors for the children. Students who graduate from high school and meet the minimum college entrance requirements are eligible to earn scholarships to USC.
- *UCS High School Internship Program.* University Computing Services (UCS) offers a six-week paid internship to 12 local high school students. Participants are chosen after consideration of recommendations submitted by high school administrators. The program provides students

with hands-on experiences designed to highlight educational opportunities and careers in computer technology. Students participate in training workshops and work within the computing facility. Divided into six separate internship cycles, the program is operational year round.

- *Upward Bound Mathematics and Science Regional Center.* In addition to the universitywide Upward Bound program, the university also offers the Upward Bound Mathematics and Science Regional Center, a three-year-old federally funded program offering intense mathematics and science instruction to 50 students. Participants reside at USC while attending classes, conducting research in laboratories, or working as interns at local corporations. Eligible students must meet Upward Bound's requirements for income and/or be potential first-generation college students. Faculty from both USC and the Los Angeles Unified School District are instructors. Students have contact with undergraduate and graduate students who are preparing to enter careers in mathematics and science.

- *USC Minority Engineering Program.* The Minority Engineering Program at USC is one of the oldest and most successful early intervention programs in California. Its aim is to recruit minority students to engineering and science programs by offering financial assistance and academic support services. Established in 1975, the program presently enrolls nearly 100 African-American, Hispanic, and American Indian students from across the country. It offers tutoring, a computer lab, opportunities for networking, financial aid, counseling, and other services, and includes a residential summer bridge program for incoming freshman and transfer students.

Community College Academic Outreach

Ever since junior colleges added vocational-technical education to their original focus on the transfer program, these two-year institutions have reached out to many constituencies in their communities. In the 1960s, public community colleges were the leaders in remedial or compensatory programs intended to bring underprepared students to collegiate academic achievement. More recently, community colleges have been active in early intervention in a wide variety of ways.

Many community colleges are now developing creative early intervention programs designed to identify students from elementary and secondary schools who lack motivation or adequate preparation for college. These programs have been designed to provide additional assistance after school or during the summer. Some have featured early placement testing paired with specialized instruction. Others are geared toward specific curricula. All of them closely link parents, partnerships with the schools, and involvement with the community (Mulder 1991, p. 33).

Often, the programs act as "bridges" and are of short duration, such as summer orientation programs. Many such activities are similar to the types of academic outreach programs offered by many four-year colleges and universities. For example, at Lake Michigan College, a community college in Benton Harbor, Michigan, inner-city high school students who have been promised scholarships to the college upon graduation are sponsored individually by volunteer faculty and staff.*

Sponsors are responsible for contacting their students at least once a month. The students spend time at the college and attend summer camps and various programs during the school year to complement their regular school activities. . . . The program has been adopted by several other community colleges in Michigan and Illinois (Mulder 1991, p. 33).

In general, however, community colleges' most outstanding contribution to early intervention and academic outreach has been in institutionalizing such efforts by establishing on-campus educational facilities and programs for youth of high school age. These initiatives are part of the school-college collaboration movement and have a wide variety of names: "2+2," middle college, urban partnership, among others. Most of the initiatives involve arrangements between a community college district and one or more local school dis-

In general, however, community colleges' most outstanding contribution to early intervention and academic outreach has been in institutionalizing such efforts by establishing on-campus educational facilities and programs for youth of high school age.

---

*See Angel and Barrera 1991, Carey, Wark, and Wellsfry 1986, Mintz 1993, and Phillips 1991 for information about specific community college outreach programs.

tricts, usually in a large metropolitan area. Some states, however, have also developed collaboration programs. An outstanding example is the Running Start program in Washington, which was mandated in 1992.

By enrolling in Running Start, eligible 11th and 12th grade students can take college-level courses at community and technical colleges for which they receive both high school and college credits, opening the possibility to receive a high school diploma and an associate's degree simultaneously. After the bill passed, a two-year pilot program was launched involving five Washington community colleges that developed and implemented the program in their districts. . . . In the fall of 1990, 358 students from 36 high schools enrolled in the pilot. Following the successful pilot project, the state's remaining 22 community colleges and five technical colleges opened their doors to Running Start students. In the fall of 1994, statewide enrollment reached 5,334 (Colwell 1995, p. 8).

The urban community colleges, however, have mainly developed academic outreach programs as school-college collaborative arrangements initiated within a metropolitan area rather than originating from state government or state-level governing or coordinating boards. These bridging programs generally fall into two categories: the "middle college" or "2+2" type (although a variety of names are used) and the urban partnership.

The concept of middle college began at La Guardia Community College in Long Island City, New York, about 20 years ago. The term "is meant to indicate 'an institution between high school and college.' Middle college high schools are essentially alternative schools for problem students, are based at colleges, and, to varying degrees, draw on the resources of the host college" (Gitman 1995, p. 6). A typical example of the La Guardia model middle college is Burlington County Alternative High School, housed in the Burlington County Community College in Pemberton, New Jersey. Students, who typically have had academic and behavioral problems in their regular high school settings, can complete their high school work on the college campus and take college courses at the same time. "The state's Department of Education is now using federal grant funds to establish similar schools linked to higher education institutions. So far, seven are based at community colleges, and negotiations are being held for other sites" (Gitman 1995, p. 6). A variation on this model is the Alternative High School Center on the campus of the Chemeketa Community College in Salem, Oregon. It has more than 100 students in grades 9 through 12 from eight local high schools.

> *Chemeketa offers a regular high school diploma, but unlike the middle colleges, many students return to their home high schools once they regain their educational foothold. The key distinction of the Chemeketa program is that its alternative students do not take college courses* (Gitman 1995, p. 7).

Although the La Guardia model was originated for "problem students" and has spawned many middle colleges with similar purposes, goals and clienteles served were diffused as the concept spread across the country. For example, Gateway High School on the campus of Gateway Community College in Phoenix, Arizona, is one of several in the Maricopa County Community College District. It currently enrolls over 200 students who are by no means predominantly "problem" students. It is simply an alternative program that allows motivated "students 16 to 21 to enter the labor force in technical and health career areas or to pursue postsecondary education" (Maricopa Community 1995, p. 1). Students can receive high school and college credits simultaneously, and it is possible for them to earn a high school diploma and an associate degree at the same time.

In Las Vegas, the Community College of Southern Nevada has joined with the local high school district to alleviate overcrowding in the rapidly growing high schools and at the same time encourage more students to earn a diploma and go on to postsecondary education. In SY 1995–96, this effort began "with 75 students at a new high school on the college's main campus" (Leahy 1996, p. A34). One motivation for the initiative is to save money by building facilities that can be shared by both the school and the college. The ultimate development of such middle colleges may blur and perhaps obliterate the distinction between high schools and community colleges.

The other principal type of school–community college collaboration that involves early intervention is the "urban partnership." The partnerships began in 1983 as a Ford Foundation–supported series of initiatives focused on alleviating problems of articulation and transfer between community colleges and four-year institutions. By 1987:

> . . . although school-college partnerships were not a formal component of the original . . . design, two-year colleges tended to collaborate with schools almost as often as they did with colleges. If more at-risk youths were eventually to receive postsecondary degrees, two-year colleges argued, it was essential to identify and support promising youngsters early (Donovan and Schaier-Peleg 1995, p. 1).

In 1988–89, school district personnel were invited to join the initiatives, and in 1991 the headquarters of the National Center for Urban Partnerships was established on the campus of Bronx Community College. One of the four tasks the center asks participating urban consortia to undertake relates directly to early intervention and academic outreach. "Teams will develop strategic plans to help significant numbers of underserved, urban students prepare for and attain postsecondary degrees" (Donovan and Schaier-Peleg 1995, p. 3).

Currently, the center sponsors partnerships in 16 cities from Seattle to Miami and from New York to Santa Ana, California. Among them is the Phoenix Think Tank, which was originally formed in 1988 "to ensure that Phoenix urban students enter, reenter, and remain in school until their maximum learning potential and goals are realized" (Beauchamp 1994, p. 10). Among the projects the Think Tank helps to coordinate is Achieving a College Education, a "2+2+2" program that articulates the junior and senior years in Phoenix high schools with freshman and sophomore years on Maricopa Community College District campuses with the upper-division baccalaureate program at Arizona State University. The Think Tank also helps coordinate Arizona State University's Hispanic Mother-Daughter Program and Upward Bound.

PROGRAM EVALUATION

In the 1992 reauthorization of the Higher Education Act of 1965, Congress recognized evaluation as the mechanism by which the worth, and eventual future, of publicly supported early intervention strategies will be determined. Consequently, assessment of early intervention programs places the educator or policy maker in a dilemma. While a positive program evaluation is powerful ammunition in the battle for funding and community support, a negative assessment can damage a program beyond repair. The lack of coordination among the varied early intervention programs has yielded operational definitions of success that vary significantly and further complicate evaluation. Consequently, evaluations of early intervention programs are rare and, for the most part, not generalizable. Upward Bound, the most extensive and widely recognized TRIO program, has been the subject of most of the these evaluations. This section presents, without critique of methodology, the findings of five evaluative studies of Upward Bound.

1. Burkheimer, Riccobono, and Wisenbaker (1979) investigated the long-term educational outcomes of participation in an Upward Bound program. Data collected through interviews, transcripts, and questionnaires yielded a positive conclusion; namely, Upward Bound is providing participating students with the tools and motivation needed for admission to and success in postsecondary education. This 1979 study is one of a series of Office of Education–sponsored reports from the Research Triangle Institute in Durham, North Carolina, that indicate the positive effects of Upward Bound.

2. Farrow, Kaplan, and Fein (1977) examined the long-term impact of the Rutgers University Upward Bound program. This longitudinal study consisted of 345 volunteers who had participated in Rutgers Upward Bound between 1966 and 1976. As part of the effort, all 345 subjects were enrolled in a college preparatory program and exposed to programs during the summer and the school year. The Rutgers Upward Bound program stressed self-concept, academic skills, and study habits. Success in college was found to be significantly greater for program participants than for nonparticipants.

3. Levine and Nidiffer (1996) reviewed the overall history and several evaluations of Upward Bound and con-

cluded that "the finding that Upward Bound has had a positive impact on college is not surprising" (p. 163). They reached this conclusion mainly because the program "telescopes or concentrates" the type of activity the student will encounter in college. They also found the opportunity for assistance by mentors a positive result but noted that the program's activities do not "generally include the group that has the largest impact on poor children—their immediate families" (p. 164). In addition to this drawback, Levine and Nidiffer stated that Upward Bound and similar "transitions" programs could be even more effective if they started with at-risk youth at an earlier age and if they served a larger portion of the potential cohort, noting that Upward Bound, by far the largest such program, reaches only "about one-fifth of the eligible population" (p. 164).

4. The National Council of Educational Opportunity Associations, a nonprofit advocacy group dedicated to expanding educational opportunity, claims that participants in Upward Bound are four times more likely to earn an undergraduate degree than students from similar backgrounds not involved in TRIO, that almost 20 percent of all African-American and Hispanic freshmen entering college in 1981 received some form of TRIO assistance, and that beneficiaries of Student Support Services are more than twice as likely to remain in college as students similarly disadvantaged not participating in the program.*

5. A 1985 study of 11 Talent Search projects concluded that proper program evaluation is extremely difficult (Hexter 1990). Amid such mixed reviews of the effectiveness of the TRIO programs, the federal government began to view access and support for at-risk students as a problem that might best be solved though increased delegation of responsibility to institutions or states.

Many obstacles face program evaluators as they attempt to study early intervention programs. Obvious pitfalls include the extended time period cohorts spend in each intervention program, varying identifications and definitions, lack of control groups, and the choice of evaluation tools. Pres-

---

* "Introducing TRIO"—NCEOA brochures 1995. Washington, D.C.

ently, few early intervention programs, save the federal initiatives, have been subject to comprehensive evaluation, but the federally mandated *National Study of Student Support Services* (Cahalan and Muraskin 1994) examines program implementation, profiles of participants, and student outcomes. The general lack of assessment is troublesome, primarily because many of today's early intervention programs have not been operational long enough to cover participants' matriculation. "Evaluation is rare, and when it does occur, it focuses on the program's process (such as how many students were served, how many pamphlets were distributed, or how many hours of counseling were supplied)" rather than on outcomes (Robyn, Klein, Carroll, and Bell 1993, p. 19). Other than those few Upward Bound evaluations mentioned earlier, the Knight Foundation, which sponsors K–16 initiatives, is another advocate of outcome-based evaluation. The foundation commissioned Policy Studies Associates in 1995 to assess the level of improvement in learning and educational opportunities derived from the school-to-college collaboration programs it sponsored as well as an ongoing program called Excellence in Education. "The evaluation found that school-college partnerships can foster *significant* improvements in educational opportunities that, in turn, contribute to greater student learning" (Policy Studies Associates 1996, p. ii). Because the projects were so varied in goals, form, and results, the evaluators found great challenges in developing a framework for consistent evaluation. The evaluators finally grouped the lessons learned from the projects according to three stages—project design, implementation, and evaluation.

Evaluations of programs that have supported students through admission to college suffer from uncoordinated definitions and identification of variables and objectives. This lack of coordination is the result of inadequate information sharing among programs, and recognition of this void (by Congress and several charitable trusts) has thus far yielded few, if any, improvements. Certainly the distinctiveness of each intervention's locale, staff, and funding affects those variables deemed worthy of assessment. For example, some programs may be designed to increase test scores, while others aim to focus on the development of healthy value systems (National Association/American Council 1989, p. 22). Consequently, evaluations focus on different aspects

Evaluations of programs that have supported students through admission to college suffer from uncoordinated definitions and identification of variables and objectives. This lack of coordination is the result of inadequate information sharing among programs, and recognition of this void has thus far yielded few, if any, improvements.

of a program. Unfortunately, comparing apples and oranges limits the impact and generalizability of the findings of analyses. Assertions based on "a motley group of interventions" produce only "average" answers and do not address the effectiveness of specific programs (Levin, Glass, and Meister 1986, p. 71).

Controlling for the external factors that contribute to a student's decision to pursue postsecondary education is difficult. Early intervention programs are populated by students with varied and often tumultuous backgrounds. Assessing the extent and influence of a student's environment on his or her educational development is at best an estimation.

The choice of methodology is more important today than ever before. The days of "feel good," pseudoscientific evaluation have given way to a new era of accountability and efficiency. If early intervention programs are to survive the times, programs must now demonstrate that they are producing results that justify the costs (Institute 1994). Chief among policy makers' and educational administrators' concerns is the cost-effectiveness of intervention programs.

When performed correctly, cost-effectiveness analysis can help guide policy makers in their allotment of resources (Levin, Glass, and Meister 1986, p. 69). Log linear analysis is a useful means to uncover complex relationships between nominally scaled data, such as those from questionnaires and surveys (Flores 1993).

Formal, accurate, and reliable evaluation of a program's effectiveness requires that rigorous criteria be met. The following guidelines are useful: (1) establish a large sample size to increase generalizability, (2) identify equivalent control and treatment groups of students, (3) determine whether students in the control group receive, from any source, services offered to the intervention group, and (4) determine whether students receive any services from outside the program that may influence their college attendance (Robyn et al. 1993). Although these guidelines clearly enhance the internal validity of evaluation, they may pose negative consequences for the individual students involved in the study. The control group, for example, may be denied valuable intervention-related services, and the treatment group may likewise be denied worthwhile services from outside the program. This dilemma is not easily resolved and requires sensitivity to the human subjects involved and to the communities served or not served by the intervention.

Another method of evaluation offers two criteria for analysis of cost-effectiveness (Levin, Glass, and Meister 1986). "First, the educational interventions that are evaluated must be readily implementable, and second, the methods used to evaluate costs and effectiveness must be acceptable" (pp. 69–70). Simply put, cost-effectiveness analysis requires researchers to study real programs that adhere to basic principles of methodology.

Through sharing information and refining methodology, early intervention advocates can combat critics with accurate and generalizable results. Coordination resulting from an increase in proper programmatic evaluation will strengthen both a program's ability to secure funding and its effect on students involved. Additionally, program administrators must recognize that, while longitudinal studies are needed, intervention requires a continuous commitment to evaluation. Exemplary approaches include the Florida Postsecondary Education Planning Commission's insightful annual evaluations of Florida's Reach-Out Program, and the Institute for Higher Education Policy's recommendation that annual funding be contingent upon annual data collected in Maryland's College Preparation Intervention Program (Institute 1994). The alternative to coordinated, comprehensive evaluation of early intervention programs is the inevitable reduction of educational opportunities for at-risk populations.

Several factors make this goal possible (Levine and Nidiffer 1996). The I Have A Dream program, for example, "reaches kids when they are young, provides enrichment activities, builds mentor teams, thinks locally, and plans individually" (p. 169). This list of factors also highlights the tremendous challenges and barriers confronting any early intervention program that hopes to be successful. One significant obstacle is the cost of effective intervention for all identified youth at risk of dropping out. By definition, such youths typically live in negative family situations and in neighborhood and school environments that inhibit the possibility of going to college. Short of canceling out the negative forces by removing the young person from the environment (which the A Better Chance program does for academically gifted minority youth at a high cost per student), where will the funds originate to overcome the negative environment? This question becomes especially pointed when applied to the cost per child over the length of time required for effective intervention. Cost estimates per child beginning at the recommended point in the early grades through the first several academic terms in college are daunting to potential benefactors in both the public and private sectors. The issue becomes particularly poignant when applied to at-risk youth of only average or below-average academic potential. Decisions about where to place scarce funds become particularly painful when they involve choices between allocating resources to increase (or at least maintain) college preparation for the masses of children in the school system or to curtail these expenditures and divert them to at-risk youth to possibly salvage them from a family, neighborhood, and school environment that portends dropping out early. Although certain programs, geared to the most needy youth, stress parental involvement as a means of enhancing family support of education and learning, the checkered history of federal and state early intervention programs suggests that, in a democratic society, the decision will favor benefiting the many rather than the few, especially when the few are located in areas where the right to vote is rarely exercised.

Countering the decision based on cost-effectiveness to continue benefiting primarily mainstream students is the awesome economic cost of *not* intervening. The costs of crime, welfare dependency, and lost tax revenue from unemployed (and unemployable) undereducated persons are well known. Not so well known, however, are the far-reaching societal consequences of not intervening. Human factors, such as anger and despair, are not as easily measured as economic factors, yet they are capable of causing great damage to the nation's psyche and to the quality of our lives. Clearly, the decisions about allocating resources involved in these issues are excruciatingly difficult.

Effective early intervention programs are prodigiously expensive because they require long-term and comprehensive efforts (see, e.g., Levine and Nidiffer 1996). Volunteer help does, of course, reduce program expenditures, but the very environment of at-risk youth contains many more negative influences than effective mentors or other role models. Given the daunting amount of financial and human resources as well as the long-term "staying power" needed for effective outcomes, it is perhaps not surprising that program evaluation is often inconclusive or, in some cases, not even undertaken in any serious cost-effective manner. But program evaluation is absolutely necessary if early intervention programs are to attract adequate initial funding and continued funding over the long haul. Perhaps program evaluation would benefit from a "global" approach that would include assessment of whether the target program is leveraging its effectiveness through coordination with other similar programs.

Evaluation based on the extent of coordination with other programs is very important (Institute 1994). "Partnerships between school districts and postsecondary institutions should form the structural backbone of any early intervention program" (p. 10). "What works" at the state level includes coordination among the principals involved; "early intervention offers a unique opportunity to coordinate many state initiatives in order to bring to fruition an increase in high school graduation rates, college enrollments, and meaningful employment among high school graduates" (p. 12).

CONCLUSIONS AND RECOMMENDATIONS

We set out to survey early intervention programs, knowing that this phenomenon of higher education is uncoordinated and rapidly expanding. We learned that the literature on this subject is amorphous, untidy, and sprawling. The limits on the length of reports in this series and the usual constraints of time and other resources mean that suitable coverage is not entirely possible of the expanding scope of early intervention and all its manifestations. Nonetheless, we believe that this work provides a preliminary conceptual framework for further study of early intervention. We chose to focus relatively more attention on state and institutional early intervention programs and somewhat less on federal and private initiatives. This choice seems reasonable after completion of this arduous review, which is still only a partial view of the field.

The federal TRIO programs still serve many constituencies after 30 years, even though serious budget cutbacks still threaten these efforts. The promising 1992 NEISP initiative was to do for early intervention what SSIG did for state-supported student financial aid, but it has been reduced to a small fraction of its intended scope. Private initiatives continue to proliferate, though apparently not at the rate of growth of the early 1980s. We can only estimate growth or decline because a comprehensive, coordinated survey would be required to compile accurate information. What is known, however, is that some private initiatives have proliferated by transformation, serving as models for many programs in the public sector. Many early intervention projects acknowledge their genesis in Lang's I Have A Dream initiative. The required survey should thus include the private initiatives that we were not able to cover in this report, including activities of national, regional, state, and even community-based foundations, as well as the vast array of professional, civic, and service organizations that provide many venues for charitable work in our society.

Limitations on the scope of and resources for this report precluded even a brief treatment of the role of business in support of early intervention. The role of business has been fairly well documented in other sources, however, such as *Corporate Support for Scholarships: A Tale of Two Cities* (Cronin 1989). We especially commend the several recent publications of the Council for Aid to Education, notably the second edition of *Business and the Schools: A Guide to Effective Programs* (Rigden 1992).

The federal TRIO programs still serve many constituencies after 30 years, even though serious budget cutbacks still threaten these efforts.

City- or metropolitan area–oriented initiatives also are not included in this report because of limited space. Such initiatives include the CollegeBound Foundation in the Baltimore area, I Know I Can in Columbus, Ohio, the Boston Plan for Excellence in the Public Schools, and Scholarships in Escrow in the Cleveland area (Robyn et al. 1993).

Among the early intervention and academic outreach programs we did include in this report, the most active and effective appear to be the burgeoning school-college collaborations. Various projects stemming from the American Association for Higher Education's initiatives in the early 1980s attracted significant foundation support and have resulted in large-scale and long-term projects across the country.

Early intervention programs are both the result of and the catalyst for an intensified focus on school-college collaboration. The rapid growth of these programs reflects the pace at which the existing gap between K–12 and higher education is closing. Current efforts at educational reform, particularly with regard to teacher education and the development of proficiency standards for students, have expanded to include a K–16 perspective. Efforts to broaden the opportunities for underrepresented minorities have also forged new and expanded partnerships between K–12 and postsecondary institutions. Early intervention programs are perhaps the foremost example of these partnerships.

Leadership for new collaborative endeavors comes from both the private and public sectors. Educational institutions, community groups, philanthropic organizations, and governmental agencies have all contributed to the growing trend toward establishing new links. In 1990, The Education Trust was established as an outgrowth of the American Association for Higher Education's Office of School/College Collaboration. Each year, The Education Trust holds a national conference in which the entire scope of American education is addressed as a single system engaged in a more coordinated process of reform.

The systemwide approach to K–16 reform has significant implications for educational administrators at the national, state, and local levels. At the local level, a network of parents, community leaders, and administrators of educational institutions must be developed to foster awareness and support of collaborative programs. With early intervention programs in particular, offerings have been so varied and uncoordinated as to impede their reaching underserved students and the dedicated educators and civic leaders who could offer valuable time and resources. Moreover, effective early intervention programs require coordination between local school districts and college and university systems, particularly with regard to admission standards, to facilitate a seamless transition from one level of education to the next. An alliance of local constituents could help articulate common goals and participate in piloting innovative services and methods of their delivery. It would also be beneficial for national, state, and local administrators to design a coordinated measure of accountability, with the aim of increasing the effectiveness of program offerings. Doing so would require the development of a basic data format that would be acceptable to participating agencies, allowing for comparative analysis as well as individualized collection of data to meet the special needs of individual communities and programs. The issue of program awareness can be dealt with nationally by creating a central clearinghouse and resource center for information, technical support, and assessment materials. It is not clear, however, who can take on this task. A report issued by the director and principal partner of The Education Trust recommends that a national "K–16 Council" be established that would promote establishment of local councils, provide a forum for dialogue and a home for research or projects of mutual interest, speak out on policy issues, and provide leadership (Haycock and Brown 1993).

Administrators on college and university campuses play a crucial role in the creation of effective school-college partnerships. By providing opportunities for K–12 students to get an early glimpse of university life, programs, and resources, the transition to higher education is rendered less daunting. For example, Arizona State University has a university transfer center, located at its largest feeder community college, that provides advisement and other needed services for prospective first-time transfer students. Perhaps the establishment of similar programs in middle schools and high schools would encourage more students to apply to college. Such encouragement is the foremost goal of early intervention programs. Student services personnel, particularly academic advisers and admissions staff, can present a clear picture of the information and competencies that students require to successfully persist through higher educa-

Administrators on college and university campuses play a crucial role in the creation of effective school-college partnerships. By providing opportunities for K–12 students to get an early glimpse of university life, programs, and resources, the transition to higher education is rendered less daunting.

tion. Once the student has reached the point of entry into college, the actual experience will seem more like a continuation than a shocking break in the continuum of education. The benefits to colleges and universities are most clearly manifested in enhanced recruitment of minority students and overall improvement in the readiness of entering freshmen.

The need for enhanced college and job readiness among America's youth was underscored with publication of *A Nation at Risk* (U.S. National Commission 1983). This document exposed the alarming trends that had already begun to significantly affect access and retention in higher education. The education pipeline was then, and is still, leaking rapidly at all levels of educational attainment, especially among low-income and minority youth.

As a result of the shrinking pool of applicants with the required preparation for higher education, a growing cohort of "conditionally admitted" students has been filling the rosters of freshmen classes. This segment of incoming freshmen needs special tutoring services and remediation efforts that have not traditionally been considered part of the mission of colleges and universities. Community colleges are often the primary source of postsecondary remedial education, but remedial English and remedial mathematics have increasingly become mainstays in all sectors of higher education. Taxpayers and legislators have raised questions about the reasons for the apparent need to twice fund high school–level education, first in the public high schools and then in the public postsecondary schools. One response to this concern is that higher education administrators have focused too intensely on the last stages in the education pipeline and have given relatively little attention to the first ones.

As suggested in the introduction, it has been widely acknowledged that efforts to increase the educational attainment of America's youth are best begun in the early grades. Administrators of colleges and universities need to establish policies and programs that take a preventive rather than curative approach to the ills afflicting the continuum of K–16 education. Many of the programs mentioned in this review provide good models for effective early intervention that focus on readiness rather than remediation. Although the list is not comprehensive, the sampling of programs offers a solid background for administrative action. University-based programs, such as those described in the section on academic outreach, provide specific models for campus-initiated efforts, such as the Hispanic Mother-Daughter Program. The good news for administrators is that a proliferation of such programs has already sprouted from a variety of private and public sources. Programs like I Have A Dream, Upward Bound, Talent Search, and Project WINGS have paved the way for leaders in higher education to contribute to and capitalize on the growing trend toward K–16 collaboration.

The proliferation of any type of social program generally proceeds in one of two manners. Programs either grow out of a coordinating organization that builds the necessary infrastructure for successful growth and maintenance, or programs proliferate unbridled and later realize the necessity for coordination. Today, early intervention efforts that grew in an uncoordinated manner have ripened to the point of harvest but are still a bit confounded by an uncertain future.

An assessment of the impact of early intervention on higher education can be considered in two dimensions. The national impact can only be determined by a large-scale, comprehensive study that would require large amounts of financial support, time, and human effort. Certainly, our work has determined that the impact of early intervention is very large, widespread, and apparently growing. Early intervention can, and probably does, affect nearly all postsecondary institutions, especially in the public sector, and one would be hard-pressed to find any public college or university without at least several students involved with a TRIO program, privately funded financial aid, or one or more of the many facets of early intervention.

It is, however, at individual institutions that the information provided in this report can be most directly applied. For example, student affairs administrators who have read this report now have a good grasp of the diversity and pervasiveness of early intervention and academic outreach programs. They probably already realize that even institution-wide academic outreach may not be coordinated through any one administrative unit. And it is quite likely that academic discipline–initiated outreach to surrounding schools is not effectively coordinated and is hence less effective than it might be. But, more important, if administrators are responsible for marketing, admissions, diversity, or minority affairs, they will soon learn that there is "good hunting" for financial aid and other types of support for at-risk students. Administrators can start by contacting local foundations, service and civic clubs, and professional organizations to learn of their involvement in early intervention efforts. Next, they should survey school districts as well as city, county, and regional agencies before turning their attention to the range of state-level entities like governing and coordinating boards and the K–12 state system. They should also direct attention to the national foundations, such as I Have A Dream in New York, or to a foundation directory that identifies project funding in this area. Finally, they should contact the national higher education associations to learn of available resources and new developments in this burgeoning field. Administrators who take these steps will benefit their institutions and help early intervention programs meet their goals of serving both students and society.

Finally, in reviewing the available information on early intervention, we were struck by the growing sense of shared responsibility for strengthening the connectedness within the entire educational process, exemplified by the mobilization and coordination of educators and administrators at all levels, as well as community leaders and legislators, in the interest of improving access to higher education. No institution or government agency can confidently assume that it can relax its efforts and that some other organization will take on the responsibility. If early intervention is to continue and advance as an effective effort, all players must develop their own role in a mutual endeavor to sustain these programs until their merit can be adequately evaluated.

APPENDIX: A Sample of Institutional Outreach Programs*

- Tuskegee University (Alabama)
  School of Nursing and Allied Health, Health and Science Scholars Program (HASSP): Provides math, science, and critical thinking enhancement activities during the summer to sixth through 11th graders in Macon County; provides exposure to health facilities and personnel through field trips and clinical rotations.

  HASSP Saturday Academy: Provides math, science, and critical thinking enrichment activities to sixth through 11th graders in Macon County throughout the academic year. Field trips to health facilities are also included.

- Wallace Community College, Selma (Alabama)
  Minority Math and Science Improvement Project: Fifty outstanding high school students were selected in 1991 to take academic courses in science and math at Alabama A&M and do internships at NASA or other high-tech industries. After completing an associate degree, the students receive a $600 summer stipend and scholarships. They then transfer to a four-year college. In 1992, another 20 students began the program.

- Northern Arizona University
  Office of Native American Programs Educational Partnerships: Elementary and secondary schools and the university form partnerships with Indian tribes.

- American River College (California)
  Partnership to Assure College Entry (PACE): Designed to keep high school students in school and to encourage them to consider college as a viable option. Provides a four-week on-campus program for a selected group of students at risk of dropping out of school but with college potential.

  Teachers of Tomorrow: Identifies potential teachers among high school students, with an emphasis on underrepresented students. Those selected for the program are given forgivable-loan scholarships and counseling to support them financially and academically through college.

- California State University–Bakersfield
  Summer Bridge Program: Four-week summer program that brings 150 first-time freshmen to campus, 94 percent of whom are nonwhite. Eighty-five percent of participants complete their degree requirement within five years.

-----

*These descriptions are taken directly, with slight edits, from Mintz 1993. Used with permission.

Career Beginnings Project: Partnership of local high schools, the university, and the private sector that focuses on reaching at-risk and low-income students before they drop out of high school; 96 percent of the students graduate from high school and 65 percent go to college. Eighty-nine percent of students served are nonwhite, 50 percent are Latino, and 60 percent are from rural high schools.

- Cosumnes River College (California)
  Program Choice: Encourages at-risk and other groups that are underrepresented in college populations to include collegiate work in their career plans; sponsors sessions to familiarize at-risk and other middle school students to the community college environment. Partnership between Cosumnes River College and the Elk Grove Unified School District.

- Pitzer College (California)
  Pitzer Early Outreach Program: Designed to motivate students to strive for postsecondary education and to help them make higher education an achievable goal. Designed to meet the needs of all students, with particular emphasis placed on encouraging African-American and Latino students to participate.

- Rancho Santiago College (California)
  College Is in My Future: Fifth grade presentations to and campus tours for minority, low-income children in the neighboring K–12 district. Local K–12 district is 94 percent ethnic minorities; 85 percent are Hispanic.

- San Jose City College (California)
  Adelante: Academic program to provide a supportive environment in which Hispanic students can achieve their goals in partnership with instructors and community mentors. Designed to increase the recruitment, educational success, and graduation rates of Hispanic students and to prepare these students for entry into the general education, occupational, and/or transfer curriculum.

- Trinidad State Junior College (Colorado)
  Cooperative Educational Services Development Association (CESDA): Seeks out minority students while in high school to encourage, motivate, and assist minorities to enroll in higher education.

- Central Florida Community College
  Project Future: Outreach program designed to reach students in grades 6 through 12 in an effort to retain, remediate, and academically enhance those who are at risk. Over a three-year period, has worked with more than 200 students from lower socioeconomic backgrounds.

- Miami-Dade Community College (Florida)
  Black Student Opportunity Program: Increases the pool of well-prepared African-American high school graduates; increases the number of African-American high school students aspiring to a college education; provides financial assistance.

  Saturday College Program: Provides tutorial support and academic enrichment to motivate and enhance the academic development of students in grades 9 through 12 in the Homestead and South Dade senior high schools. Facilitates the progress of targeted high school participants to enable them to earn an associate degree or a four-year degree, or acquire technical skills by exposing them to community people who have achieved academic goals.

- Indiana University/Purdue University at Fort Wayne
  FAST Program (Future Academic Scholars Track): Since 1987, helps African-American, Hispanic, and at-risk children prepare for higher education.

- Manchester College (Indiana)
  College Vision Program: Focuses on influencing young minority students from junior and senior high school to stay in school and think and plan toward a college education; special efforts to prepare students for success in the college setting through seminars and workshops offered just prior to the beginning of their college career; incorporates a mentor program.

- Wabash College (Indiana)
  Alliance for Raising Educational Achievement (AREA): Partnership of public school systems, historically black colleges and universities, liberal arts institutions, and universities to improve education across the educational system from kindergarten to postgraduate study and to stimulate and encourage young people from underrepresented groups to complete their education through college and graduate school.

  Wabash College/Washington High School Bridge Program: Cooperative program to encourage and prepare educationally disadvantaged pupils to attend college.

- Dillard University (Louisiana)
  Concentrated Academic Program: Four-year concentrated academic program in local high schools for at-risk students with academic potential; increases access of students to higher education; recruitment begins in ninth grade through 12th grade.

- Regis College (Massachusetts)
  College Awareness Program: Since 1987, targets talented Boston-area Hispanic students about to enter ninth grade; promotes the advantages of higher education to Hispanic students; and educates students and their parents about college financial aid and admission processes.

- Western New England College (Massachusetts)
  Educational Opportunity Program: Invites at-risk junior high school and high school students to interact with the college's students of color while being encouraged to finish school and go on to college.

- University of Missouri–Kansas City
  Chancellor's Minority Scholar Banquet: Introduces minority students to the quality of instruction and the broad range of academic disciplines the university provides. Motivates students to pursue higher education.

  Greater Kansas City Hispanic Youth Day: Increases Hispanic high school students' level of awareness regarding career alternatives/selection, postsecondary educational opportunities, available financial aid, and scholarships.

- Dona Ana Branch Community College (New Mexico)
  Concurrent Enrollment Program: Articulated between area high schools and the college, allows high school seniors to complete high school graduation requirements while enrolled in and completing a community college vocational certificate–level program. The opportunity to allow students to attend college without paying tuition has opened the door to students who may not have previously considered any postsecondary education.

- Case Western Reserve University (Ohio)
  Career Beginnings: Two-year intervention program for at-risk high school juniors and seniors. Matches students with a teacher, minister, and business or professional mentor who helps the students solve practical problems, develop skills, locate opportunities, and make career plans; presents workshops on study and community skills, career planning, college admission, and financial aid; offers participants meaningful summer jobs in the public and private sector.

- University of Toledo (Ohio)
  Toledo Excel: Serves minority students in the Toledo metropolitan area, giving them success and access to higher education. Each year 50 minority eighth graders are promised full scholarships to the uni-

versity if they follow a prescribed college preparatory program.

- Pennsylvania State University–Allentown
  Academic Enrichment and Recruitment Program for Youth with Special Academic and Career Needs: Enables 43 at-risk minority students from eighth through 11th grades to become qualified for admission to the institution upon graduation; involves community agencies, local industry, and continuing education and resident instruction faculty.

- Southwest Texas State University
  Youth Opportunities Unlimited: Academic and vocational summer residential program for economically disadvantaged 14- and 15-year-olds at risk of dropping out of the secondary school system.

- University of Houston (Texas)
  Yates Partnership: University African-American male students are paired with African-American male Yates senior high students to provide high school students with mentoring and tutoring services. Goal is to increase the number of African-American males continuing their education beyond high school.

- University of North Texas
  University Outreach Program: Designed to help African-American and Hispanic students prepare for university-level academic work. Operates under the philosophy that the best solution to problems such as minority undereducation is to address these issues at the public school level by encouraging students not only to graduate from high school but also to consider college as well. Established in 1987, with the University of Texas and Texas A&M.

- Madison Area Technical College (Wisconsin)
  Minority Precollegiate Program: In an effort to deal with the problems faced by secondary school minority populations, a pilot project was developed by the college, in cooperation with area colleges and universities, to provide minority high school seniors with additional classroom instruction, work experience through part-time jobs, and an orientation to postsecondary educational institutions through campus visits. Students completing the program are prepared to either pursue postsecondary studies or enter the job market.

REFERENCES

The Educational Resources Information Center (ERIC) Clearinghouse on Higher Education abstracts and indexes the current literature on higher education for inclusion in ERIC's database and announcement in ERIC's monthly bibliographic journal, *Resources in Education* (RIE). Most of these publications are available through the ERIC Document Reproduction Service (EDRS). For publications cited in this bibliography that are available from EDRS, ordering number and price code are included. Readers who wish to order a publication should write to the ERIC Document Reproduction Service, 7420 Fullerton Road, Suite 110, Springfield, Virginia 22153-2852. (Phone orders with VISA or MasterCard are taken at 800/443-ERIC or 703/440-1400.) When ordering, please specify the document (ED) number. Documents are available as noted in microfiche (MF) and paper copy (PC). If you have the price code ready when you call, EDRS can quote an exact price. The last page of the latest issue of *Resources in Education* also has the current cost, listed by code.

Advisory Committee on Student Financial Assistance. 1993. "Early Eligibility Determinations." Briefing paper. Washington, D.C.: Author. ED 357 692. 15 pp. MF–01; PC–01.

American Association for Higher Education. October 1995. *Accelerating Reform in Tough Times: Focus on Student Learning K–16 Program.* AAHE 6th National Conference on School/College Collaboration. Washington D.C.: Author.

Angel, D., and A. Barrera, eds. 1991. *Rebuilding Minority Enrollment.* New Directions for Community Colleges No. 74. San Francisco: Jossey-Bass.

Arnold, Karen D. 1995. *Lives of Promise: What Becomes of High School Valedictorians. A Fourteen-Year Study of Achievement and Life Choices.* San Francisco: Jossey-Bass.

Ascher, Carol. 1988. *School and College Collaboration: A Strategy for Helping Low-Income Minorities.* New York: ERIC Clearinghouse on Urban Education. ED 308 258. 46 pp. MF–01; PC–02.

Barbic, Craig. May 1997. "AISES Precollege Program Information." Online: *http://www.colorado.edu/AISES/precoll.htm*

Beauchamp, Janet. 1994. *Exploring Best Practices.* 2d ed. Phoenix: Phoenix Think Tank.

Boyer, Ernest L. 1993. "Ready to Learn: A Mandate for the Nation." *Young Children* 48(3): 54–57.

Brod, Pearl. 1970. "Effects of Tutoring on the Tutee in an Upward

Bound Program." Paper presented at the 1970 Annual Meeting of the American Personnel and Guidance Association, New Orleans, Louisiana. ED 132 442. 9 pp. MF–01; PC–01.

Brown, Nevin. Fall 1994. "Community Compacts: Models for Metropolitan Universities." *Metropolitan Universities: An International Forum* 5(2): 25–31.

Burd, Stephen, and Karla Haworth. 16 May 1997. "Students Would Receive New Tax Breaks and Larger Pell Grants under the Budget Deal." *Chronicle of Higher Education:* A26–27.

Burkheimer, G.J., Jr., J.A. Riccobono, and J.M. Wisenbaker. 1979. *Evaluation Study of the Upward Bound Program: A Second Follow-up.* Final report. Durham, N.C.: Research Triangle Institute. ED 186 574. 570 pp. MF–03; PC not available EDRS.

Cahalan, Margaret, and Lana Muraskin. 1994. *National Study of Student Support Services.* Interim report. Vol. 1, *Program Implementation.* Washington, D.C.: U.S. Dept. of Education. ED 370 512. 359 pp. MF–01; PC–15.

Cardenas, Raul, and Elizabeth Warren. 1991. "Community College Access: Barriers and Bridges." In *Rebuilding Minority Enrollment,* edited by D. Angel and A. Barrera. New Directions for Community Colleges No. 74. San Francisco: Jossey-Bass.

Carey, Diane, Linda Wark, and Norval Wellsfry. 1986. "Partnerships for Excellence: High Schools and Community Colleges." Sacramento: Association of California Community College Administrators. ED 278 433. 23 pp. MF–01; PC–01.

Cepeda, Rita. 1993. "Report on the California Middle College–High School Program." Los Angeles: Board of Governors of the California Community Colleges.

Chaney, Bradford, Laurie Lewis, and Elizabeth Farris. 1995. *Programs at Higher Education Institutions for Disadvantaged Precollege Students.* NCES 96-230. Washington, D.C.: U.S. Government Printing Office. ED 391 437. 106 pp. MF–01; PC–05.

Coleman, James S. 1966. "Equal Schools or Equal Students?" *The Public Interest* 4: 70–75.

Coles, Larry. 1995a. *Making Equity Central to the Board: A Process for Change.* New York: College Board.

———. 1995b. *Ready, Set, Go.* New York: College Board.

College Board. 1994a. *Creating a National Equity Agenda: First Lessons from EQUITY 2000.* New York: Author.

———. 1994b. *EQUITY 2000: What It Takes Creating a Supportive Climate for Implementation.* New York: Author.

———. 1995. *Trends in Student Aid: 1985 to 1995.* Washington, D.C.: Author.

Colwell, Lynn H. June/July 1995. "Two Degrees for the Price of One." *Community College Journal:* 8–10.

Committee on Education and Labor. 1992. *Higher Education Amendments of 1992.* Report No. 102–447. Washington, D.C.: U.S. House of Representatives.

Council of Chief State School Officers. May 1997. "Resource Center on Educational Equity."

Cronin, Joseph M. 1989. *Corporate Support for Scholarships: A Tale of Two Cities.* Boston: Massachusetts Higher Education Assistance Corporation. ED 312 925. 34 pp. MF–01; PC–02.

Davis, Jerry S. 1989a. "Junior High School Students' Interest in 'Early Awareness' Program Activities." *Journal of Student Financial Aid* 19(2): 4–14.

——. 1989b. *The Role of Parents and Their Preferences in Junior High School Students' Postsecondary Plans.* Harrisburg: Pennsylvania Higher Education Assistance Agency.

——. 1991. *Do Early Awareness Programs Have Early Effects?* Harrisburg: Pennsylvania Higher Education Assistance Agency.

DeWitt Wallace–*Reader's Digest* Fund. 1996. *Setting Change in Motion: 1995 Annual Report.* New York: Author.

Donovan, Richard, and Barbara Schaier-Peleg. 1995. "Overview." New York: National Center for Urban Partnerships.

Duffus, Lee R., and Madelyn L. Isaacs. 1991. "Minority Education Intervention: The Experience of Two Programs with Middle and High School Students and Their Families." Paper presented at the Breivogel Conference, Fort Myers, Florida.

Duncan, Greg J., and Willard L. Rogers. 1985. "A Demographic Analysis of Childhood Poverty." Cited by Congressional Research Service in *Children in Poverty.* Washington, D.C.: U.S. House of Representatives.

Farrow, Earl V., Lawrence Kaplan, and Bernard Fein. 1977. *Long-Term Impact of the Rutgers Upward Bound Program on Its Participants.* New Brunswick, N.J.: Rutgers University.

Fenske, Robert H., and Brian D. Gregory. 1994. "The Dream Denied? Evaluating the Impact of Student Financial Aid on Low-Income and Minority Students." In *Advances in Program Evaluation, Vol. 2,* edited by Henry T. Frierson. Boston: JAI Press.

Flores, Antonio. 1993. "Early Awareness Strategies and Their Measurement." Paper presented at the 1993 Annual Conference of the National Association of Student Financial Aid Administrators, San Diego, California. ED 370 518. 23 pp. MF–01; PC–01.

Florida Postsecondary Education Planning Commission. 1994. *A Statewide Evaluation of Florida's College Reach-Out Program.*

Tallahassee: Author. ED 382 753. 79 pp. MF–01; PC–04.

Freeman, Ernest T. 1989. "Report on Early Awareness." Paper presented at the Sixth Annual NASSGP/NCHELP Research Network Conference, Boston, Massachusetts.

Gill, Judith L. 1991. *The Road to College: Educational Progress by Race and Ethnicity.* Boulder, Colo.: Western Interstate Commission for Higher Education.

Gitman, Mitch. 16 January 1995. "Alternative High Schools Find Success on Community College Campuses." *Community College Week:* 6–8.

Gladieux, Larry E., and R.D. Reischauer. 4 September 1996. "High Tuition, More Grade Inflation." *Washington Post.*

Gomez, Manual N., J. Bissell, L. Danziger, and R. Casselman. 1990. *To Advance Learning: A Handbook on Developing K–12 Postsecondary Partnerships.* New York: University Press of America.

Gomez, Manual N., and Alfredo de los Santos. 1992. *An Analysis of State Policies for Fostering and Sustaining Collaboration: Critical Underpinnings of Educational and Social Policies for the 21st Century.* Denver: Education Commission of the States.

Green, Patricia, and Leslie Scott. 1995. "'At-Risk' Eighth Graders Four Years Later." NCES 95-736. Washington D.C.: U.S. Government Printing Office. ED 386 496. 13 pp. MF–01; PC–01.

Greenberg, Arthur A. 1991. *High School–College Partnerships.* ASHE-ERIC Higher Education Report No. 5. Washington, D.C.: George Washington Univ., Graduate School of Education and Human Development. ED 343 546. 125 pp. MF–01; PC–05.

Gross, Thomas L. 1988. *Partners in Education.* San Francisco: Jossey-Bass.

Haggstrom, Gus W., Thomas J. Blaschke, and Richard J. Shavelson. 1991. *After High School, Then What?* Santa Monica, Calif.: Rand Corporation. ED 360 512. 185 pp. MF–01; PC–08.

Halcon, John J. 1988. *Exemplary Programs for College-Bound Minority Students.* Boulder, Colo.: Western Interstate Commission for Higher Education. ED 298 830. 47 pp. MF–01; PC not available EDRS.

Haycock, Kati. January/February 1996. "Thinking Differently about School Reform." *Change:* 13–18.

Haycock, Kati, and Nevin Brown. 1993. "Higher Education and the Schools: A Call to Action and a Strategy for Change." Washington, D.C.: American Association for Higher Education. ED 369 356. 12 pp. MF–01; PC–01.

Hexter, Holly. 1990. *A Description of Federal Information and Outreach Programs and Selected State, Institutional, and Com-*

munity Models. Washington, D.C.: U.S. Government Printing Office. ED 357 686. 75 pp. MF–01; PC–03.

Hoffer, Thomas B., Kenneth A. Rasinski, and Whitney Moore. 1995. "Social Background Differences in High School Mathematics and Science Coursetaking and Achievement." NCES 95-206. Washington, D.C.: U.S. Government Printing Office. ED 389 533. 18 pp. MF–01; PC–01.

Hossler, Don, and Frances K. Stage. 1992. "Family and High School Experience Influences on the Postsecondary Educational Plans of Ninth Grade Students." *American Educational Research Journal* 29(2): 425–51.

Institute for Higher Education Policy. 1994. "Statewide Early Intervention Programs: What Works." *Policy Steps* 2(1): 1–12.

———. 1995. "Welfare Reform: Impacting Educational Opportunity." *Policy Steps* 2(3): 1–12.

Jones, Vinneta. 1994. "Lessons from the EQUITY 2000 Education Reform Model." New York: College Board.

Kennedy, Mary M., Richard K. Jung, and Martin E. Orland. 1986. *Poverty, Achievement, and the Distribution of Compensatory Education Services.* Interim report. Washington, D.C.: U.S. Dept. of Education. ED 71 546. 344 pp. MF–01; PC–14.

Lacey, Richard A. 1991. "'I Have a Dream' for Dropout Prevention." *Education Digest* 56(20): 20–23.

Leahy, Patrick. 16 February 1996. "A Community College Meets Big Demand in Las Vegas." *Chronicle of Higher Education:* A34.

Lederman, Douglas. 8 August 1997. "Budget Deal Gives Students and Colleges the Biggest Infusion of U.S. Aid in Decades." *Chronicle of Higher Education:* A28.

Levin, Henry M., Gene V. Glass, and Gail Meister. September 1986. "The Political Arithmetic of Cost-Effectiveness Analysis." *Phi Delta Kappan:* 69–72.

Levine, Arthur, and Jana Nidiffer. 1996. *Beating the Odds: How the Poor Get to College.* San Francisco: Jossey-Bass.

Lewenstein, Phil. 1995. "The Minnesota National Early Intervention Scholarship and Partnership Program." Saint Paul: Minnesota Higher Education Services Office.

Long, Cynthia D. 1996. "Nota Bene." *Academe* 82(1): 6.

McLain, John. 1996. *The National Early Intervention Scholarship and Partnership Program.* Olympia, Wash.: Higher Education Coordinating Board.

Maricopa Community College District. October/November 1995. "Youths Thrive at New Gateway High." *Ed Cetera:* 1+.

Merisotis, Jamie P., and Jeneva E. Burroughs. 1994. *Evaluation of* the *College Preparation Intervention Program: A Report to the Maryland Higher Education Commission.* Washington, D.C.: Institute for Higher Education Policy.

Millard, Richard M. 1991. *Today's Myths and Tomorrow's Realities.* San Francisco: Jossey-Bass.

Miller, John W. 1992. "Students at Risk: Pitfalls and Promising Plans." Paper presented at the Third Annual Conference on Students at Risk, Savannah, Georgia.

Mingle, James R., and Esther Rodriguez, eds. 1990. *Building Coalitions for Minority Success: A Report of the SHEEO Project on Minority Achievement.* Denver: State Higher Education Executive Officers. ED 331 908. 65 pp. MF–01; PC not available EDRS.

Mintz, Suzanne D. 1993. *Sources: Diversity Initiatives in Higher Education.* Washington, D.C.: American Council on Education.

Mortenson, Thomas G. 1990. *The Reallocation of Financial Aid from Poor to Middle-Income and Affluent Students, 1978 to 1990.* Iowa City: American College Testing Program. ED 319 312. 75 pp. MF–01; PC–03.

———. 1991. *Equity of Higher Educational Opportunity for Women, Black, Hispanic, and Low-Income Students.* Iowa City: American College Testing Program. ED 328 133. 141 pp. MF–01; PC–06.

Mulder, Anne E. 1991. "Minority Student Recruitment." In *Rebuilding Minority Enrollment,* edited by D. Angel and A. Barrera. New Directions for Community Colleges No. 74. San Francisco: Jossey-Bass.

National Association of Student Financial Aid Administrators. 1988. *Pilot Projects: Reports and Compendium of Early Awareness Programs in the United States.* Washington, D.C.: Author.

———. 1994. *Early Awareness Resource Guide.* Washington, D.C.: Author.

National Association of Student Financial Aid Administrators/ACE. 1989. *Certainty of Opportunity: A Report on the NASFAA/ACE Symposium on Early Awareness of Postsecondary Education.* Washington, D.C.: Author. ED 317 644. 40 pp. MF–01; PC–02.

National Center for Education Statistics. 1994a. *The Condition of Education, 1994.* NCES 94-149. Washington, D.C.: U.S. Government Printing Office. ED 371 491. 475 pp. MF–01; PC–19.

———. 1994b. *Digest of Education Statistics, 1994.* NCES 94-115. Washington, D.C.: U.S. Government Printing Office. ED 377 253. 584 pp. MF–03; PC–24.

———. 1995a. *The Condition of Education, 1995.* NCES 95-273. Washington, D.C.: U.S. Government Printing Office. ED 383

119. 547 pp. MF–02; PC–22.

———. 1995b. *Digest of Education Statistics, 1995.* NCES 95-029. Washington, D.C.: U.S. Government Printing Office. ED 387 885. 604 pp. MF–03; PC–25.

———. 1996a. *The Condition of Education, 1996.* NCES 96-304. Washington, D.C.: U.S. Government Printing Office. ED 394 217. 411 pp. MF–01; PC–17.

———. 1996b. *Digest of Education Statistics, 1996.* NCES 96-133. Washington, D.C.: U.S. Government Printing Office.

National Commission on Responsibilities for Financing Post-secondary Education. 1993. *Making College Affordable Again.* Washington, D.C.: Author. ED 351 995. 103 pp. MF–01; PC–05.

National Council of Educational Opportunity Associations. April 1997. "NCEOA." *Opportunity Outlook:* i.

Oakes, Jennie. 1990. *Multiplying Inequalities: The Effects of Race, Social Class, and Tracking on Opportunities to Learn Mathematics and Science.* Santa Monica, Calif.: Rand Corporation. ED 329 615. 152 pp. MF–01; PC not available EDRS.

Perna, Laura W. 1995. "Early Intervention Programs: A New Approach to Increasing College Access." Paper presented at the 12th Annual NASSGP/NCHELP Research Network Conference, Minneapolis, Minnesota.

Perry, George, and Nancy Kopperman. 1973. *A Better Chance: Evaluation of Student Attitudes and Academic Performance, 1964–1972.* New York: Alfred P. Sloan Foundation.

Phillips, Roy G. 1991. "Model Programs in Minority Access." In *Rebuilding Minority Enrollment,* edited by D. Angel and A. Barrera. New Directions for Community Colleges No. 74. San Francisco: Jossey-Bass.

Policy Studies Associates. 1996. *Learning to Collaborate: Lessons from School-College Partnerships in the Excellence in Education Program.* Miami: John S. and James L. Knight Foundation.

Quality Education for Minorities Project. 1990. *Education That Works: An Action Plan for the Education of Minorities.* Cambridge: Massachusetts Institute of Technology.

Richmond, George. 1990. "The Student Incentive Plan: Mitigating the Legacy of Poverty." *Phi Delta Kappan* 72(3): 227–29.

Riehl, Richard J. Fall 1994. "The Academic Preparation, Aspirations, and First-Year Performance of First-Generation Students." *College and University:* 14–17.

Rigden, Diana W. 1992. *Business and the Schools: A Guide to Effective Programs.* New York: Council for Aid to Education.

Robyn, Abby E., S.P. Klein, S.J. Carroll, and S.J. Bell. 1993.

Programs to Promote College Attendance That Combine Services and Financial Aid. Santa Monica, Calif.: Rand Corporation. ED 360 886. 70 pp. MF–01; PC–03.

Rose, Richard B. Spring/Summer 1993. "Resources for Early Intervention Strategies." *College and University:* 68–72.

Rubin, C. 1990. "Early Awareness: A Strategy That Improves Secondary School Academic Preparation and Postsecondary Access." *American Secondary Education* 18(4): 23–25.

St. John, Edward P., and Jay Noell. 1989. "The Effects of Student Financial Aid on Access to Higher Education: An Analysis of Progress with Special Consideration of Minority Enrollment." *Research in Higher Education* 30(6): 563–81.

Schwartz, Samuel, and Sandra Baum. 1989. "Some New Evidence on the Determinants of Student Loan Default." In *Proceedings for the NASSGP/NCHELP Research Network,* edited by J.S. Davis. Harrisburg: Pennsylvania Higher Education Assistance Authority.

Scott, Leslie A., Donald A. Rock, Judith M. Pollack, and Steven J. Ingels. 1995. *Two Years Later: Cognitive Gains and School Transitions of NELS:88 Eighth Graders. National Educational Longitudinal Study of 1988.* NCES 95-436. Washington, D.C.: U.S. Government Printing Office. ED 391 844. 277 pp. MF–01; PC–12.

Seppanen, Loretta. 1991. *The Running Start Program: Impact and Benefits from the First Year in Washington Community Colleges.* Olympia: Washington State Board for Community and Technical Colleges. ED 338 288. 52 pp. MF–01; PC–03.

Smith, James P. 1995. "Racial and Ethnic Differences in Wealth in the Health and Retirement Study." *Journal of Human Resources* 30: 158–83.

Smith, Thomas M. 1995a. *The Educational Progress of Black Students: Findings from* The Condition of Education, 1994. NCES 95-765. Washington, D.C.: U.S. Government Printing Office.

———. 1995b. *The Educational Progress of Hispanic Students: Findings from* The Condition of Education, 1995. NCES 95-767. Washington, D.C.: U.S. Government Printing Office.

Stoel, Carol, Wendy Togneri, and Patricia Brown. 1992. *What Works: School/College Partnerships to Improve Poor and Minority Student Achievement.* Washington, D.C.: American Association for Higher Education.

Stout, Robert T. 1990. "Early Intervention Strategies: University Efforts to Identify and Nurture Minority Students." *Metropolitan Education* 11(3): 25–36.

U.S. Bureau of the Census, U.S. Department of Commerce. 1988.

Household Wealth and Asset Ownership, 1988. Washington, D.C.: U.S. Government Printing Office.

———. 1993. *Population Projections of the United States by Age, Sex, Race, and Hispanic Origin, 1993–2050.* Washington, D.C.: U.S. Government Printing Office.

———. 1994. *Income, Poverty, and Valuation on Noncash Benefits, 1994.* Current Population Reports, Series P-60. Washington, D.C.: U.S. Government Printing Office.

U.S. Department of Education. 1995. *Application for State Grants under the National Early Intervention Scholarship and Partnership (NEISP) Program.* Washington, D.C.: Author.

U.S. Department of Labor. 1994. *Employment Status of School-Age Youth, High School Graduates, and Dropouts.* Washington, D.C.: Author.

U.S. National Commission on Excellence in Education. 1983. *A Nation at Risk: The Imperative for Educational Reform.* A report to the nation and the Secretary of Education. Washington, D.C.: Author. ED 226 006. 72 pp. MF–01; PC–03.

U.S. Senate. 1991. Hearings on Early Intervention. Washington, D.C.: U.S. Government Printing Office.

U.S. Senate, Committee on Labor and Human Resources. 1991. "Access to Higher Education: Increasing Pell Grants and Widening Opportunities." Washington, D.C.: Author.

Wallace, Jennifer. 1993. *Building Bridges: A Review of the Middle School–College Partnership Literature.* Denver: Education Commission of the States. ED 365 199. 27 pp. MF–01; PC–02.

Whiteley, Meredith A., and Eleanor C. Lacy. 1985. "Demographics of Minority Student Recruitment, Arizona State University." Tempe: Arizona State Univ., Office of Institutional Planning and Analysis.

Wilbur, Franklin P., and Leo M. Lambert, eds. 1996. *Linking America's Schools and Colleges: Guide to Partnerships and National Directory.* 2d ed. Washington, D.C.: American Association for Higher Education.

Williamson, Madeline J. 1995. "The Seamless Web: Mentoring Minority Students through the Academic Pipeline from High School to Community College to Baccalaureate Transfer and through Graduate Degree Attainment." Unpublished manuscript. Tempe: Arizona State University, Graduate College.

Wolanin, Thomas P. April 1997. "The History of TRIO: Three Decades of Success and Counting." *Opportunity Outlook:* 2–4.

Zook, Jim. 9 June 1995. "Threatened by the Budget Ax: Lobbying for Survival, TRIO Programs Point to Success Stories." *Chronicle of Higher Education:* A26.

INDEX

A

AAHE. *See* American Association for Higher Education

academic achievement and courses taken, 18–22

Academic Enrichment and Recruitment Program for Youth with
    Special Academic and Career Needs, 91

"academic outreach," 8

    homepage on the World Wide Web, 58

    of the urban institutions as three possible types, 57

    program benefits, 9

    two types, 9

accelerated programs offering college-level instruction, 37

ACE. *See* Achieving a College Education

Achieving a College Education, 60, 72

ACPE. *See* Arizona Commission for Postsecondary Education

Adelante, 88

Advanced Placement program, 37

AFDC. *See* Aid to Families with Dependent Children

African-Americans

    children average expected years in poverty, 13

    junior and senior high school students

        mentoring program aimed at male, 64

    report in 1994 on, 19–20

    students gap with whites exists even after African-American
        students have dropped out, 20

    Student Opportunity Program, 89

Aid to Families with Dependent Children

    mothers who enter postsecondary educational programs
        could lose welfare support, 16–17

AISES. *See* American Indian Science and Engineering Society

Algebridge, 62

Alliance for Raising Educational Achievement, 89

Alternative High School Center

    on campus of Chemeketa Community College in Salem
        Oregon, 71

American Association for Higher Education, 37–38, 82

    Education Trust outgrowth of Office of School/College
        Collaboration of, 82

American Association for the Advancement of Science, 40

American Council on Education, 14

    directory of college and university programs for historically
        underrepresented students, 58

American Indian population

Montana project tracking system focused on students in its, 39

American Indian Science and Engineering Society, 32

American River College (California)
    institutional outreach programs of, 87

analysis of cost-effectiveness criteria, 77

A Nation at Risk
    exposed alarming trends affecting access and retention in higher education, 84
    responses to, 20–21

Angel and Barrera 1991: for information on community college outreach programs, 69

AP. *See* Advanced Placement program

AREA. *See* Alliance for Raising Educational Achievement

Arizona
    Commission for Postsecondary Education, 49
    General Accounting Office review of Upward Bound programs, 74
    Mathematics, Engineering, Science Achievement, 62
    Minority Education Access and Achievement Cooperative, 39
    Student Program Investing Resources for Education, 49-50
        modeled after IHAD, 30

Arizona State University, x, 72
    differences with regard to outreach from the University of Southern California, 60
    outreach programs at, 60–64
    university transfer center, 83

Asian -Americans students
    complete more math and science courses within all socioeconomic categories than other groups, 21

ASPIRE. *See* Arizona Student Program Investing Resources for Education

at-risk eight grader students characteristics, 14

B

Baltimore area
    CollegeBound Foundation in the, 82

Basic Educational Opportunity Grant program, 2
    as authorized in 1972 were to provide a "floor" of gift aid, 22

Benton Harbor, Michigan, 69

A Better Chance, 30–31
    results in removal from negative family situations, 78

Birmingham, Alabama has
    Community Compacts for Student Success project, 38
Blacks. *See* Afro Americans.
Boston Plan for Excellence in the Public Schools, 82
BRIDGES. *See* Building Relationships to insure Greater Educational
    Success
Bronx Community College, 72
Brooklyn College
    actively engaged in outreach programs for minority youth, 56
Building Relationships to Insure Greater Educational Success, 66
Burkheimer, Riccobono, and Wisenbaker (1979)
    investigated the long-term educational outcomes of
        participation in an Upward Bound program, 73
Burlington County Community College in Pemberton New Jersey
    as example of middle college, 70–71
Business and the Schools: A Guide to Effective Programs, 81
business role in support of early intervention, 81

C

California
    Early Intervention Scholarship and Partnership Program
        in, 46
    General Accounting Office review of Upward Bound
        programs, 74
    NEISP program in, 46
California State University at Dominguez Hills, 57
    actively engaged in outreach programs for minority youth, 56
California State University-Bakersfield
    collaboration with the public sector, especially with school
        systems and local community colleges fostered by, 58
    institutional outreach programs of, 87–88
Career Beginnings Project, 87–88, 90
Carey, Wark, and Wellsfry 1986: for information on specific
    community college outreach programs, 69
Carnegie Corporation, 27
Carnegie Foundation, 31
Carroll, Donna, xi
Case Western Reserve University (Ohio)
    institutional outreach programs of, 90
CEAS. *See* College of Engineering and Applied Sciences
Center for Gifted and Talented Native Hawaiian children, 50
central clearing house and resource center for information,
    issue of program awareness dealt with by, 83

Central Florida Community College
    institutional outreach programs of, 88
CESDA. *See* Cooperative Educational Services Development
    Association
Chancellor's Minority Scholar Banquet, 90
Chemeketa Community College in Salem Oregon
    Alternative High School Center, 71
Children's Crusade for Higher Education of Rhode Island, 47
Child Care Action Campaign, 40
city or metropolitan area-oriented initiatives, 82
Civil Rights Act of 1964, 6
Cleveland area
  Scholarships in Escrow in the, 82
Coalition to Increase Minority Degrees, 63
Coleman findings called attention to family and neighborhood
    influences on educational achievement, 5
collaboration
        programs between community college district and local
            school district, 69–70
        with the public sector, especially with school systems
            and local community colleges, fostered by university, 58
college attendance, rising cost of, 23
College Awareness Program, 90
College Board, 37
        EQUITY 2000 as educational initiative of, 31
CollegeBound Foundation in the Baltimore area, 82
college degree may be as necessary for economic security
        as a high school diploma was not long ago, 1–2
college graduates have high employment rates, income, and
        occupational status, 17–18
College Is in My Future, 88
College of Engineering and Applied Sciences, 63
College Preparation Intervention Program of Maryland, 46–47
College Preparatory Schools Program, 30
College Vision Program, 89
Colorado focusing on system that accurately tracks students, 39
Columbus Ohio,
        "I Know I Can" is in, 82
Commission on Higher Education 1947 report, 2
Community College
        Academic Outreach, 68–72
        of Southern Nevada joined with local Las Vegas high school
            district to alleviate overcrowding, 71

        outreach programs information, 69
Community Compacts for Student Success project, 38
Concentrated Academic Program, 89
"concurrent-enrollment models," 37
Concurrent Enrollment Program, 64, 90
"conditionally admitted" students filling the roster of freshmen
        classes, 84
Condition of Education, 6
        in 1994 focused on African-American and Hispanic stu-
        dents, 19
Cooperative Educational Services Development Association, 88
Corporate Support for Scholarship: A Tale of Two Cities', 81
cost-effectiveness
        analysis, 77
        of intervention programs, 76
Cosumnes River College (California)
        institutional outreach programs of, 88
Council for Aid to Education
        recommend recent publications of, 81
Council of Chief State School Officers, 39–40
Cuomo, New York Governor, 51
Current Population Surveys of March 1992
        dropouts more likely to be unemployed and be on
            welfare, 16

D

defaulters on student loans, 24
Delta Kappa Gamma Society International local chapter
        Project WINGS founded by, 32–33, 33
demographic issues and early intervention, 9–13
Department of Education
        responsible for informing the public of eligibility require-
        ments
        for TRIO and financial awards, 41
DeWitt Wallace-*Reader's Digest* Foundation, 27, 32
Dillard University (Louisiana)
        institutional outreach programs of, 89
directory of college and university programs
        American Association for Higher Education, 58–59
        American Council on Education, 58
DOE. See Department of Education
Dona Ana Branch Community College (New Mexico)
        institutional outreach programs of, 90

"dreamers," 28

dropouts, 14

 and educational attainment, 13–16

 as one of the country's most serious and persistent
  problems, 14

 not only more likely to be unemployed but *also* much
  more likely to be on welfare, 16

DuBrock, Caryl, xi

E

"early awareness," 8

"early eligibility," 8

"early intervention," 7

 foundation awards related to, 27

 four main elements of federal definition of, 8

 impact on higher education considered in two
  dimensions, 85

 problems and issues addressed by, 9

 Scholarship and Partnership Program in California, 46

Early Intervention Programs

 as a way for institutions to add value to their communities, ix

 Implications for College and University Administrators, v–vi

 seven goals for, 44

 six forms of, iv–v

 three critical constituencies for, 44

 to stimulate interest in careers, ix

 traditional reason for, ix

early intervention strategies evaluation

 for determining if worth publicly supporting, 73

"early outreach" as example of

 unilateral academic outreach program, 58

Educational

 Consolidation and Improvement Act, 12

 Excellence for Children with Environmental Limitations, 67

 Opportunity Centers, 42, 43

 Opportunity Grants, 22

 Opportunity Program, 90

 Talent Search Program, 64

Education Commission of the State, 36, 38–39

Education Support Centers, 41

Education Trust, 38, 82

 report recommends a national "K-16 Council," 83

Electronic Need Analysis System, 41

Elementary and Secondary Education Act of 1965, 6, 12
El Paso Texas Community Compacts for Student Success project, 38
Entrepreneur Program
      in USC's School of Business Administration, 66
EOCs. *See* Educational Opportunity Centers
EQUITY 2000, 30–31
ESEA. See Elementary and Secondary Education Act
Estimator, 41
ETSP. *See* Educational Talent Search Program
evaluation
      as the mechanism for determining worth of publicly
         supported early intervention strategies, 73
      guidelines for determination of program effectiveness, 76–77
EXCEL, 62
Excellence in Education
      assessed by Policy Studies Associates in 1995, 75
Expected Family Contribution Formula Book: The Counselor's
      Handbook for High Schools, 41
Exploration of Architecture, 66

F

FAAP. See Financial Aid and Academic Planning
Faculty Ambassadors, 60–61
family and neighborhood
      negative influences on educational achievement of, 12
Family Development Institute, 65
Family Support Act of 1988, 17
Farrow, Kaplan, and Fein (1977): examined long-term impact of
      Rutgers University Upward Bound program, 73
FAST Program (Future Academic Scholars Track), 89
Federal and State Cost Sharing Programs, 43–44
federal financial assistance shift from grant aid to loans, 22
Fife, Jon, xi
Financial Aid and Academic Planning, 61
Florida State University
      actively engaged in outreach programs for minority youth, 56
Florida General Accounting Office
      review of Upward Bound programs, 74
Florida current-enrollment program, 37
Florida International University
      actively engaged in outreach programs for minority youth, 56
      works closely with community minority advocacy groups
         on recruiting minority youth, 58

Florida Postsecondary Education Planning Commission
annual evaluation of Florida's Reach-Out Program, 77
Ford Foundation, 27, 31
"urban partnership" as begun as series of initiatives
supported by, 72
Fort Worth Texas
EQUITY 2000 initiated its approach in, 32
Freshman Scholars Program, 52
funding sources for individual institutions, 85–86
Future Start in Vermont, 47–48

G

GAO. *See* General Accounting Office
Gateway High School on campus of Gateway Community College
in Phoenix Arizona, 71
General Accounting Office 1974 evaluation of Upward Bound
contradicts many earlier and subsequent positive
studies, 73–74
Georgia
General Accounting Office reviewed Upward Bound
programs, 74
HOPE program, 44
GI Bill of 1944, 5
"global approach"
program-evaluation might benefit from, 79
Greater Kansas City Hispanic Youth Day, 90
Great Society legislation of the mid-1960s, 6
Grinnell College in Iowa took full responsibility for sponsorship
and developing program and support services for IHAD
project, 30
"guaranteed-tuition programs," 8
guidelines for formal, accurate and reliable evaluation of
program effectiveness, 76–77

H

Hanson, Carol, xi
Hartford, Connecticut
Community Compacts for Student Success project, 38
HASSP. *See* School of Nursing and Allied Health, Health and
Science Scholars Program
Hawaii's Hope and related programs, 50–51
Hawaiian Opportunity Program in Education program, 44, 50–51

HEA. *See* Higher Education Act of 1965
Higher Education Act of 1965, 2, 6
        initiated major federal programs for student financial
            assistance, 2
Higher Education Act 0f 1965 as reauthorized in 1992, 7, 43
        evaluation as mechanism determining worth of publicly
            supported early intervention strategies, 73
Higher Education Act 0f 1965 as reauthorized in 1997, 43
Higher Education Amendments of 1986, 43
Higher Learning Access Program, 53
High School and Beyond longitudinal study, 15
high school students
        enter as transfer students rather than first-time freshmen, 64
Hispanic Mother-Daughter Program, 61, 72, 85
Hispanic students, 19-20
HOPE. *See* Hawaiian Opportunity Program in Education
Houston Endowment, 27
HSB. *See* High School and Beyond longitudinal study

I
"I can dream it, I can do it," 47
IHAD. *See* I Have A Dream Foundation
I Have A Dream Foundation, 28–30
        parent involvement is crucial in projects, 28
        program, 3, 77–78, 85
        program of Lang, Eugene, 49
"I Know I Can" in Columbus Ohio, 82
Illinois project focus attention on
        "transfer points," 39
Implications for College and University Administrators
        of Early Intervention Programs, v–vi
Indiana
        NEISP program, 46
        Twenty-First Century Scholars Program, 46
Indiana University-Purdue University at Fort Wayne
        institutional outreach programs, 89
individual institution impact of
        early intervention on higher education, 85–86
Institute for Social Research of University of Michigan, 13
Institute of Higher Education recommended that College
        Preparation Intervention Program funding be contingent
            upon annual data, 77

Integrated Postsecondary education data System, 55

J

JEP. *See* Joint Educational Project
Job Opportunities Basic Skills program, 17
JOBS. See Job Opportunities Basic Skills program
John S. and James L. Knight Foundation, 27
Joint Educational Project, 64–65

K

"K-16 Council," recommendation of a national, 83
K-16 Movement, 35–37
Kellogg Foundation, 27
Knight Foundation which sponsors K-16 initiatives
        is another advocate of outcome based evaluation, 75
KUSC (USC's radio station), 67

L

La Guardia Community College in long Island City, New York
        middle college concept began at, 70
La Guardia model originated for "problem students," 71
Lake Michigan College, 69
Lang, Eugene, 28
        I Have A Dream program of, 49
Lang's I Have A Dream initiative
        many early intervention projects acknowledge genesis in, 81
leadership in school-college collaboration by state-level higher
        education governing boards, support of, 39
Legislative College Opportunity Program, 52
Levin, Henry, 15
Levine and Nidiffer (1996): review of history and evaluation of
        Upward Bound success, 74
Liberty program modeled after I Have A Dream, 30
Livingston Middle School in New Orleans, 51
log linear analysis as a useful means to uncover complex
        relationships between nominally scaled data, 76
Los Angeles Unified School District, 68
Louisiana's TAYLOR program, 51
low-income/minority students
        likely to be reluctant to borrow for education, 24

M

Madison Area Technical College (Wisconsin)

institutional outreach programs of, 91
Manchester College (Indiana)
　　institutional outreach programs of, 89
Manoa campus of University of Hawaii, 50
Maricopa County
　　Community College District, 64, 72
　　on-campus visits to high schools of, 62
Marketplace in the Schools, 67
Maryland
　　College Preparation Intervention Program, 46–47
　　　　funding suggest contingent upon annual data, 77
　　NEISP program in, 46–47
Massachusetts
　　General Accounting Office review of Upward Bound
　　　　programs, 74
　　project focus attention on "transfer points," 39
mathematics concentration of EQUITY 2000, 30
Mathematics, Engineering, Science Achievement, 67
Math-Science Honors Program, 63
"mediation," 56
Memphis State University, 58
　　actively engaged in outreach programs for minority
　　　　youth, 56
　　collaboration with the public sector, especially with school
　　systems and local community colleges, fostered by, 58
MEP. *See* Summer Bridge Minority Engineering Program
MESA. *See* Arizona Mathematics, Engineering, Science Achievement
Miami-Dade Community College (Florida)
　　institutional outreach programs of, 89
middle colleges, 69
　　began at La Guardia Community College, 70
　　may blur distinction between high schools and community
　　　　colleges, 71
Milwaukee Wisconsin EQUITY 2000 site, 32
Minnesota
　　NEISP program, 47
　　current-enrollment program, 37
　　Education Services Office, 46–47
Minority
　　children non-school deficiency is pervasive, 6
　　Math and Science Improvement Project, 87
　　Parents Outreach Committee, 62
　　Precollegiate Program, 91

Mintz 1993: A Sample of Institutional Outreach Programs, 91
    for information on specific community college outreach
        programs, 69
Montana project tracking system
    focused on students in its American Indiana population, 39

N

NAEP. *See* National Assessment of Educational Progress
Na Pua No'eau statewide outreach program, 50
NASFAA. See National Association of Student Financial Aid
    Administrators
Nashville, Tennessee EQUITY 2000 site, 32
National Assessment of Educational Progress
    tracked achievement levels, 19
National Association of Student Financial Aid Administrators, 14
National Center for Education Statistics, 55
National Center for Urban Partnerships, 72
National Council of Educational Opportunity Associations, 42, 74
National Early Intervention Scholarship and Partnership program.
    See NEISP
National Educational Longitudinal Study of 1988, 14, 19, 21
national impact of early intervention impact on higher education, 85
National Science Foundation, 31, 32
National Study of Student Support Services, 75
A Nation at Risk, 37–38
NCEOA. *See* National Council of Educational Opportunity
    Association
negative family situations, removal from, 78
Neighborhood Academic Initiative, 65
NEISP, 41, 43–44
    initiative of 1992, 81
    mission statement of, 7
    State Implementation of, 44–49
NELS:88. *See* National Educational Longitudinal Study of 1988
Nevada
    General Accounting Office review of Upward Bound
        programs, 74
New Hampshire
    General Accounting Office review of Upward Bound
        programs, 74
New Mexico NEISP program, 47
New York City area current-enrollment programs, 37
New York's Liberty Scholarship and Partnership Program, 51–52

        modeled after I Have a Dream, 30
New York Tuition Assistance Program, 52
nonminority youth relative decline, 56–57
Norman Topping Student Aid Fund, 65
North Carolina's Legislative College Opportunity Program, 52
Northern Arizona University institutional outreach programs, 87
Norwood, Cristie, xi
NTSAF. *See* Norman Topping Student Aid Fund

O
Office of Education-sponsored reports, 73
Office of Native American Programs Educational Partnerships, 87
Office of School/College Collaboration, 38
Oklahoma's Higher Learning Access Program, 53
on campus educational facilities and programs for youth of high
        school age, 69
101 Black Men of America, 64
Operation Manong, 50
Outreach Program, 65
overcrowding
        Community College of Southern Nevada joined with local
            Las Vegas high school district to alleviate, 71

P
PACE. *See* Partnership to Assure College Entry
parent involvement in I Have a Dream projects is crucial, 28
Parents as Partners, 61
Partnership to Assure College Entry, 87
Peer Counseling Program, 65
Pell grants. See Basic Educational Opportunity Grant program
Pennsylvania State University-Allentown
        institutional outreach programs of, 91
Philadelphia, Pennsylvania
        Community Compacts for Student Success project, 38
Phillips 1991: for information on specific community college
        outreach programs, 69
Phillips Academy in Andover Massachusetts, 30
Phoenix Think Tank, 72
Pitzer College (California)
        institutional outreach programs of, 88
        Early Outreach Program, 88
Policy Studies Associates commissioned to assess level of
        improvement in learning and educational opportunities, 75

POP. *See* Promise of Progress

"postures" that assist in successfully recruiting and graduating minority youth, 57

poverty
    annual income connection with minority status , 10–11
    close relationship with achievement in school, 6

"poverty-impacted" schools
    drag down achievement of both poor and nonpoor children, 12

PPS. *See* Parents as Partners

Pre-College Summer Art Program, 67

precollegiate program for disadvantaged students
    survey of, 55–59
    top three goals of, 56

Pre-Freshman Enrichment Project, 50

PREP. *See* Pre-Freshman Enrichment Project

Preparing Your Child for College: A Resource Book for Parents, 41

Prince Georges County, Maryland EQUITY 2000 site, 32

prison costs for one year more than four years of college costs, 15

"problem students"
    La Guardia model originated for, 71

Program Choice, 88

program effectiveness
    guidelines for formal, accurate and reliable evaluation, 76–77

program evaluators
    problems of, 75

Project Advance, 37

Project Future, 88

Project WINGS, 32–33, 85
    distinctive small-scale early intervention program, 32

Promise of Progress, 64

proprietary vo-tech schools
    attending students default at a high rate on the loans needed to meet the relatively high tuition, 3

Providence, Rhode Island
    Community Compacts for Student Success project, 38
    EQUITY 2000 site, 32

Pueblo, Colorado
    Community Compacts for Student Success project, 38

R

race differences in wealth are enormous, 11

Rancho Santiago College (California)

institutional outreach programs of, 88

Rand Corporation national survey, 11

Reach-Out Program annual evaluation
    by Florida Postsecondary Education Planning
        Commission, 77

Regis College (Massachusetts)
    institutional outreach programs of, 90

Research and Development Program, 65

Research Triangle Institute in Durhan North Carolina, 73

Resource Center on Educational Equity, 39

Retention Program, 65

Rhode Island
    Children's Crusade for Higher Education, 47
    NEISP program in, 47
    review of Upward Bound programs in, 74

Rio Salado Community College, 64

Rockefeller Foundation, 31

Ronald E. McNair Postbaccalaureate Achievement Program, 41, 42

Running Start program in Washington
    statewide community college collaboration program, 70

Rutgers University Upward Bound program
    Farrow, Kaplan, and Fein (1977) examined long-term
        impact, 73

S

San Jose, California EQUITY 2000 site, 32

San Jose City College (California)
    institutional outreach programs of, 88

Saturday College Program, 89

Scholarships in Escrow in the Cleveland area, 82

School, College, and University Partnership Program, 43

"school-college collaboration" as a major theme of educational
        reform movement, 35

school-college partnerships, 38-39
    annotated bibliography on, 38
    can foster significant improvements in educational
        opportunities, 75

school dropouts cost, 15

School of Nursing and Allied Health, Health and Science
        Scholars, 87
    Saturday Academy, 87

schools with large proportions of poor students, 12

SCOAR. *See* Student Committee on Admissions and Recruitment

SCUPP. *See* School, College, and University Partnership Program

Seamless Web, 61

"seamless web" model, 36

SHEEO. See State Higher Education Executive Officers

Sias, Betsy, xi

societal consequences of not intervening
    less well known but potentially significant, 78

Southwest Texas State University
    institutional outreach programs of, 91

SSIG. See State Student Incentive Grant program

SSS. See Student Support Services

Stanford University in California, 15
    took full responsibility for sponsorship and developing
        program
    and support services for I Had a Dream project, 30

State Higher Education Executive Officers, 39

State Implementation of NEISP, 44–49

State leadership for Schools and Colleges Partnerships, 38–39

State Student Incentive Grant program, 44
    initiative, 81

statewide community college collaboration program
    Running Start program in Washington, 70

"staying power" required long-term for effective outcomes, 79

Student Aid Tour, 41

Student Committee on Admissions and Recruitment, 65–66

student financial aid and college costs, 22–25

Student Support Services, 41, 42
    National Study of, 75
    claim that beneficiaries more than twice as likely to
        remain in college, 74
    offers tutoring and support, 43

Success Express, 62

"success story" of 1980 sophomores showed strong correlation's
    with socioeconomic status and race/ethnicity, 15–16

Summer Bridge
    Minority Engineering Program, 63
    Program, 87

summer orientation programs, 69

Sun Devil Summer Bridge Program, 63

Super Enrichment Saturdays, 50

Survey on Precollegiate Programs for Disadvantaged Students at
    Higher Education Institutions, 55

Syracuse University's Project Advance, 37

T

Talent Search, 41, 42, 56, 85
 example of unilateral academic outreach program, 57
 federal program, 7
 identifies promising students, 43
 program evaluation is extremely difficult, 74–75
tax code as a support for higher education, 25
TAYLOR program, 51
Teachers of Tomorrow, 87
"telescopes or concentrates" type of activity student will encounter
 in college, 74
Tempe Union high schools, 64
Temple University
 actively engaged in outreach programs for minority
  youth, 56
 collaboration with the public sector, 58
 works closely with community minority advocacy groups, 58
Testskills, 62
Todd, Kimberly, xi
Toledo Excel, 90–91
Traditional Separation between K-12 and Higher Education, 35
Training Program for Special Services Staff and Leadership, 41
"transfer points," 39
Trinidad State Junior College (Colorado)
 institutional outreach programs of, 88
TRIO programs, 41
 could be effected by 1997 reauthorization of the Higher
  Education Act, 43
Truman Commission. See Commission on Higher Education 1947
 report
Tuskegee University (Alabama) institutional outreach programs, 87
Twenty-First Century Scholars Program, Indiana, 46
"2+2," 69
"2+2+2" program, 72

U

UCLA, 58
 actively engaged in outreach programs for minority youth, 56
 collaboration with the public sector, especially with school
 systems and local community colleges fostered by, 58
 works closely with community minority advocacy groups
  on common goals of recruiting minority youth, 58
UH. See University of Hawaii

Undergraduate admissions projects, 62
unilateral academic outreach program
        talent searches as example of, 57
University Computing Services (UCS), 67–68
universal access to college education as a "dream denied," 25
University of California at Los Angeles. See UCLA
University of Hawaii, 50
University of Houston (Texas) institutional outreach programs, 91
University of Michigan Institute for Social Research, 13
University of Missouri-Kansas City
        Institutional outreach programs of, 90
University of New Mexico
        actively engaged in outreach programs for minority youth, 56
University of North Carolina, 52
University of North Texas
        institutional outreach programs of, 91
University of Southern California
        differences with regard to outreach from Arizona State
            University, 60
        High School Internship Program, 67–68
        Minority Engineering Program, 68
        outreach programs at the, 64–68
        Precollege Enrichment Academy, 65
University of Texas at El Paso
        actively engaged in outreach programs for minority youth, 56
University of Toledo (Ohio) institutional outreach programs, 90–91
University of Vermont, 44
University Outreach Program, 91
university transfer center of Arizona State University, 83
Upward Bound, 31, 41–42, 62, 66, 72, 85
        Mathematics and Science Regional Center, 68
        negative 1974 evaluation, 73–74
        participants four times more likely to earn an
            undergraduate degree, 74
        positive effects of, 73
        prepared for the rigors of college-level academic work, 43
        six evaluative studies of, 73–79
        success because "telescopes or concentrates" type of
            activity student will encounter in college, 74
urban partnership, 69
        as another type of school-community college
            collaboration, 72
USC. See University of Southern California

U. S. Department of Education, 55

V

Vermont
        Future Start, 47–48
        General Accounting Office review of Upward Bound
            programs, 74
        NEISP program in, 47–48
        Student Assistance Corporation, 47

W

Wabash College (Indiana) institutional outreach programs of, 89
Wabash College/Washington High School Bridge Program, 89
Wallace Community College, Selma (Alabama)
        institutional outreach programs of, 87
War on Poverty
        resulted in expanded access and support for populations
        previously underrepresented on college campuses, 41
Washington NEISP program, 48
Washington State Higher Education Coordinating Board, 48
Wayne State University, 57
        actively engaged in outreach programs for minority
            youth, 56
wealth, enormous differences in race differences in, 11
welfare system designed to support single mothers who lost
        husbands during World War II, 16
"welfare-to-work" tax credit in spring 1997, 17
Western New England College (Massachusetts)
        institutional outreach programs of, 90
white children, many live in poverty and also are at risk to fall in
        educational system, 13
white-minority gap in academic achievement no longer closing, 19
white poverty tends as temporary (especially for students), 11–12
Wibbing, Eric, xi
Wisconsin NEISP program, 48
WISE. See Women in Applied Science and Engineering
Wise Investment in the Next Generation of Students. See Project
        WINGS
Women in Applied Science and Engineering, 63–64
Wright, Cherri, xi

Y

Yale University in New Haven Connecticut

organizing I Had a Dream project, 30
Yates Partnership, 91
YEP. *See* Young Entrepreneur Program
Young Entrepreneur Program, 66
Youth Opportunities Unlimited, 91

ASHE-ERIC HIGHER EDUCATION REPORTS

Since 1983, the Association for the Study of Higher Education (ASHE) and the Educational Resources Information Center (ERIC) Clearinghouse on Higher Education, a sponsored project of the Graduate School of Education and Human Development at The George Washington University, have cosponsored the ASHE-ERIC Higher Education Report series. This volume is the twenty-fifth overall and the eighth to be published by the Graduate School of Education and Human Development at The George Washington University.

Each monograph is the definitive analysis of a tough higher education problem, based on thorough research of pertinent literature and institutional experiences. Topics are identified by a national survey. Noted practitioners and scholars are then commissioned to write the reports, with experts providing critical reviews of each manuscript before publication.

Eight monographs (10 before 1985) in the ASHE-ERIC Higher Education Report series are published each year and are available on individual and subscription bases. To order, use the order form on the last page of this book.

Qualified persons interested in writing a monograph for the ASHE-ERIC Higher Education Report series are invited to submit a proposal to the National Advisory Board. As the preeminent literature review and issue analysis series in higher education, the Higher Education Reports are guaranteed wide dissemination and national exposure for accepted candidates. Execution of a monograph requires at least a minimal familiarity with the ERIC database, including *Resources in Education* and the current *Index to Journals in Education*. The objective of these reports is to bridge conventional wisdom with practical research. Prospective authors are strongly encouraged to call Dr. Fife at 800/773-3742.

For further information, write to
    ASHE-ERIC Higher Education Reports
    The George Washington University
    One Dupont Circle, Suite 630
    Washington, DC 20036
Or phone (202) 296-2597; toll free: 800-773-ERIC.

Write or call for a complete catalog.

Visit our Web site at **www.gwu.edu/~eriche**

ADVISORY BOARD

James Earl Davis
University of Delaware at Newark

Cassie Freeman
Peabody College–Vanderbilt University

Susan Frost
Emory University

Mildred Garcia
Arizona State University West

James Hearn
University of Georgia

Philo Hutcheson
Georgia State University

Laura W. Perna
Frederick D. Patterson Research
  Institute of the College Fund/UNCF

Steven G. Olswang
University of Washington

Brent Ruben
State University of New Jersey–Rutgers

Sherry Sayles-Folks
Eastern Michigan University

Daniel Seymour
Claremont College–California

Pamela D. Sherer
The Center for Teaching Excellence

Marilla D. Svinicki
University of Texas–Austin

David Sweet
OERI, U.S. Department of Education

Gershon Vincow
Syracuse University

W. Allan Wright
Dalhousie University

Donald H. Wulff
University of Washington

Manta Yorke
Liverpool John Moores University

REVIEW PANEL

Charles Adams
University of Massachusetts–Amherst

Louis Albert
American Association for Higher Education

Richard Alfred
University of Michigan

Henry Lee Allen
University of Rochester

Philip G. Altbach
Boston College

Marilyn J. Amey
University of Kansas

Kristine L. Anderson
Florida Atlantic University

Karen D. Arnold
Boston College

Robert J. Barak
Iowa State Board of Regents

Alan Bayer
Virginia Polytechnic Institute and State University

John P. Bean
Indiana University–Bloomington

John M. Braxton
Peabody College, Vanderbilt University

Ellen M. Brier
Tennessee State University

Barbara E. Brittingham
The University of Rhode Island

Dennis Brown
University of Kansas

Peter McE. Buchanan
Council for Advancement and Support of Education

Patricia Carter
University of Michigan

John A. Centra
Syracuse University

Arthur W. Chickering
George Mason University

Darrel A. Clowes
Virginia Polytechnic Institute and State University

Cynthia S. Dickens
Mississippi State University

Deborah M. DiCroce
Piedmont Virginia Community College

Sarah M. Dinham
University of Arizona

Kenneth A. Feldman
State University of New York–Stony Brook

Dorothy E. Finnegan
The College of William & Mary

Mildred Garcia
Montclair State College

Rodolfo Z. Garcia
Commission on Institutions of Higher Education

Kenneth C. Green
University of Southern California

James Hearn
University of Georgia

Edward R. Hines
Illinois State University

Deborah Hunter
University of Vermont

Philo Hutcheson
Georgia State University

Bruce Anthony Jones
University of Pittsburgh

Elizabeth A. Jones
The Pennsylvania State University

Kathryn Kretschmer
University of Kansas

Marsha V. Krotseng
State College and University Systems of West Virginia

George D. Kuh
Indiana University–Bloomington

Daniel T. Layzell
University of Wisconsin System

Patrick G. Love
Kent State University

Cheryl D. Lovell
State Higher Education Executive Officers

Meredith Jane Ludwig
American Association of State Colleges and Universities

Dewayne Matthews
Western Interstate Commission for Higher Education

Mantha V. Mehallis
Florida Atlantic University

Toby Milton
Essex Community College

James R. Mingle
State Higher Education Executive Officers

John A. Muffo
Virginia Polytechnic Institute and State University

L. Jackson Newell
Deep Springs College

James C. Palmer
Illinois State University

Robert A. Rhoads
The Pennsylvania State University

G. Jeremiah Ryan
Harford Community College

Mary Ann Danowitz Sagaria
The Ohio State University

Daryl G. Smith
The Claremont Graduate School

William G. Tierney
University of Southern California

Susan B. Twombly
University of Kansas

Robert A. Walhaus
University of Illinois–Chicago

Harold Wechsler
University of Rochester

Elizabeth J. Whitt
University of Illinois–Chicago

Michael J. Worth
The George Washington University

RECENT TITLES

Volume 25 ASHE-ERIC Higher Education Reports

1. A Culture for Academic Excellence: Implementing the Quality Principles in Higher Education
   Jann E. Freed, Marie R. Klugman, and Jonathan D. Fife

2. From Discipline to Development: Rethinking Student Conduct in Higher Education
   Michael Dannells

3. Academic Controversy: Enriching College Instruction through Intellectual Conflict
   David W. Johnson, Roger T. Johnson, and Karl A. Smith

4. Higher Education Leadership: Analyzing the Gender Gap
   Luba Chliwniak

5. The Virtual Campus: Technology and Reform in Higher Education
   Gerald C. Van Dusen

Volume 24 ASHE-ERIC Higher Education Reports

1. Tenure, Promotion, and Reappointment: Legal and Administrative Implications (951)
   Benjamin Baez and John A. Centra

2. Taking Teaching Seriously: Meeting the Challenge of Instructional Improvement (952)
   Michael B. Paulsen and Kenneth A. Feldman

3. Empowering the Faculty: Mentoring Redirected and Renewed (953)
   Gaye Luna and Deborah L. Cullen

4. Enhancing Student Learning: Intellectual, Social, and Emotional Integration (954)
   Anne Goodsell Love and Patrick G. Love

5. Benchmarking in Higher Education: Adapting Best Practices to Improve Quality (955)
   Jeffrey W. Alstete

6. Models for Improving College Teaching: A Faculty Resource (956)
   Jon E. Travis

7. Experiential Learning in Higher Education: Linking Classroom and Community (957)
   Jeffrey A. Cantor

8. Successful Faculty Development and Evaluation: The Complete Teaching Portfolio (958)
   John P. Murray

Volume 23 ASHE-ERIC Higher Education Reports

1. The Advisory Committee Advantage: Creating an Effective Strategy for Programmatic Improvement (941)
   Lee Teitel

2. Collaborative Peer Review: The Role of Faculty in Improving College Teaching (942)
   Larry Keig and Michael D. Waggoner

3. Prices, Productivity, and Investment: Assessing Financial Strategies in Higher Education (943)
   Edward P. St. John

4. The Development Officer in Higher Education: Toward an Understanding of the Role (944)
   Michael J. Worth and James W. Asp II

5. Measuring Up: The Promises and Pitfalls of Performance Indicators in Higher Education (945)
   Gerald Gaither, Brian P. Nedwek, and John E. Neal

6. A New Alliance: Continuous Quality and Classroom Effectiveness (946)
   Mimi Wolverton

7. Redesigning Higher Education: Producing Dramatic Gains in Student Learning (947)
   Lion F. Gardiner

8. Student Learning outside the Classroom: Transcending Artificial Boundaries (948)
   George D. Kuh, Katie Branch Douglas, Jon P. Lund, and Jackie Ramin-Gyurnek

Volume 22 ASHE-ERIC Higher Education Reports

1. The Department Chair: New Roles, Responsibilities, and Challenges (931)
   Alan T. Seagren, John W. Creswell, and Daniel W. Wheeler

2. Sexual Harassment in Higher Education: From Conflict to Community (932)
   Robert O. Riggs, Patricia H. Murrell, and JoAnne C. Cutting

3. Chicanos in Higher Education: Issues and Dilemmas for the 21st Century (933)
   Adalberto Aguirre Jr., and Ruben O. Martinez

4. Academic Freedom in American Higher Education: Rights, Responsibilities, and Limitations (934)
   Robert K. Poch

5. Making Sense of the Dollars: The Costs and Uses of Faculty Compensation (935)
   Kathryn M. Moore and Marilyn J. Amey

6. Enhancing Promotion, Tenure, and Beyond: Faculty Socialization as a Cultural Process (936)
   William G. Tierney and Robert A. Rhoads

7. New Perspectives for Student Affairs Professionals: Evolving Realities, Responsibilities, and Roles (937)
   Peter H. Garland and Thomas W. Grace

8. Turning Teaching into Learning: The Role of Student Responsibility in the Collegiate Experience (938)
   Todd M. Davis and Patricia Hillman Murrell

Volume 21 ASHE-ERIC Higher Education Reports

1. The Leadership Compass: Values and Ethics in Higher Education (921)
   John R. Wilcox and Susan L. Ebbs

2. Preparing for a Global Community: Achieving an International Perspective in Higher Education (922)
   Sarah M. Pickert

3. Quality: Transforming Postsecondary Education (923)
   Ellen Earle Chaffee and Lawrence A. Sherr

4. Faculty Job Satisfaction: Women and Minorities in Peril (924)
   Martha Wingard Tack and Carol Logan Patitu

5. Reconciling Rights and Responsibilities of Colleges and Students: Offensive Speech, Assembly, Drug Testing, and Safety (925)
   Annette Gibbs

6. Creating Distinctiveness: Lessons from Uncommon Colleges and Universities (926)
   Barbara K. Townsend, L. Jackson Newell, and Michael D. Wiese

7. Instituting Enduring Innovations: Achieving Continuity of Change in Higher Education (927)
   Barbara K. Curry

8. Crossing Pedagogical Oceans: International Teaching Assistants in U.S. Undergraduate Education (928)
   Rosslyn M. Smith, Patricia Byrd, Gayle L. Nelson, Ralph Pat Barrett, and Janet C. Constantinides

ORDER FORM

Quantity

Amount

_____ Please begin my subscription to the current year's *ASHE-ERIC Higher Education Reports* (Volume 25) at $120.00, over 33% off the cover price, starting with Report 1. _____

_____ Please send a complete set of Volume ___ *ASHE-ERIC Higher Education Reports* at $120.00, over 33% off the cover price. _____

Individual reports are available for $24.00 and include the cost of shipping and handling.

SHIPPING POLICY:

- Books are sent UPS Ground or equivalent. For faster delivery, call for charges.
- Alaska, Hawaii, U.S. Territories, and Foreign Countries, please call for shipping information.
- Order will be shipped within 24 hours after receipt of request.
- Orders of 10 or more books, call for shipping information.

All prices shown are subject to change.

Returns: No cash refunds—credit will be applied to future orders.

PLEASE SEND ME THE FOLLOWING REPORTS:

Quantity	Volume/No.	Title	Amount

Please check one of the following:
- ☐ Check enclosed, payable to GW-ERIC.
- ☐ Purchase order attached.
- ☐ Charge my credit card indicated below:
  - ☐ Visa ☐ MasterCard

Subtotal: _____

Less Discount: _____

Total Due: _____

Expiration Date_____

Name_____

Title_____

Institution_____

Address_____

City _____ State _____ Zip_____

Phone _____ Fax _____ Telex_____

Signature _____ Date_____

**SEND ALL ORDERS TO: ASHE-ERIC Higher Education Reports
The George Washington University
One Dupont Cir., Ste. 630, Washington, DC 20036-1183
Phone: (202) 296-2597 • Toll-free: 800/773-ERIC
FAX: (202) 452-1844
URL: www.gwu.edu/~eriche**